POLAND

CHRISTIAN PARMA
photography

RENATA GRUNWALD-KOPEĆ
text

Wydawnictwo PARMA® PRESS

POLAND

Poland covers 312,685 km², making it the world's 63rd largest country and Europe's 9th largest. Territorial waters extend over 8700 km², while the Vistula and Szczecin Lagoons cover 1200 km². The country's nearly 39 million inhabitants are 96% Polish, 4% ethnic minorities – mainly Germans, Byelorussians and Ukrainians. The official language is Polish, the currency the złoty (of which 1 is made up of 100 groszy). The country is a pluralistic democracy with a parliament elected by universal suffrage every four years. 460 deputies sit in its Sejm or lower house, 100 senators in its Senat. The President of the Republic is in turn elected every 5 years. The legal foundations of the Third Republic of Poland are as set out in the Constitution of April 2nd 1997.

The emblem of Poland is a white eagle in a golden crown facing right, with a golden beak and claws, set against a red rectangular field. The Polish colours are red and white and these are arranged horizontally on the country's flag, with white above and red below.

An Act entering into force on January 1st 1999 ushered in a new territorial division of the state, into 16 voivodships (province-regions), 315 poviats ("counties") plus 65 towns with poviat rights and 2489 urban, urban-rural, and rural.

The nation's capital is Warsaw.

The Polish calendar includes 11 public holidays, which are either national commemorations (Labour Day – May 1st, Constitution Day – May 3rd and Independence Day – November 11th) or days of religious significance (two days at Easter, Corpus Christi, August 15th – the holiday of the Assumption of the Virgin Mary, November 1st – All Saints Day, December 25th and 26th – Christmas Day and Boxing Day), plus January 1st – New Year's Day.

THE HISTORY OF POLAND — p. 4

POLAND'S GEOGRAPHY — p. 6

1 ZACHODNIOPOMORSKIE — SZCZECIN
VOIVODSHIP — CAPITAL — p. 8

2 POMORSKIE — GDAŃSK
VOIVODSHIP — CAPITAL — p. 14

3 KUJAWSKO-POMORSKIE — BYDGOSZCZ
VOIVODSHIP — CAPITAL — p. 20

4 WARMIŃSKO-MAZURSKIE — OLSZTYN
VOIVODSHIP — CAPITAL — p. 26

5 PODLASKIE — BIAŁYSTOK
VOIVODSHIP — CAPITAL — p. 32

6 MAZOWIECKIE — WARSZAWA
VOIVODSHIP — CAPITAL — p. 40

7 ŁÓDZKIE — ŁÓDŹ
VOIVODSHIP — CAPITAL — p. 50

8 WIELKOPOLSKIE — POZNAŃ
VOIVODSHIP — CAPITAL — p. 58

9 LUBUSKIE — GORZÓW WLKP.
VOIVODSHIP — CAPITAL — p. 68

10 DOLNOŚLĄSKIE — WROCŁAW
VOIVODSHIP — CAPITAL — p. 74

11 OPOLSKIE — OPOLE
VOIVODSHIP — CAPITAL — p. 86

12 ŚLĄSKIE — KATOWICE
VOIVODSHIP — CAPITAL — p. 92

13 ŚWIĘTOKRZYSKIE — KIELCE
VOIVODSHIP — CAPITAL — p. 98

14 LUBELSKIE — LUBLIN
VOIVODSHIP — CAPITAL — p. 104

15 PODKARPACKIE — RZESZÓW
VOIVODSHIP — CAPITAL — p. 110

16 MAŁOPOLSKIE — KRAKÓW
VOIVODSHIP — CAPITAL — p. 116

THE HISTORY OF POLAND

Bolesław the Brave (967-1025).

Kazimierz the Great (1310-1370).

Władysław Jagiełło (1348-1434).

Zygmunt III Waza (1566-1632).

At the end of the first millennium A.D., a considerable part of Europe was inhabited by Slav tribes. The land that is now Poland belonged to the Western Slavs, including the Wiślanie (Vistulanian) tribe inhabiting the area around what is now Kraków, and the Polanie (Polanians) living around today's Gniezno. In the 10th century, the Polanians managed to unite some of the tribes under the ruling Piast family, and it was they who would go on to rule Poland for four centuries. In 966, one of their number – Duke Mieszko I – took baptism and initiated a new chapter in the history of Poland; whose full sovereignty as a country was confirmed during a meeting of Bolesław "the Brave" with Holy Roman Emperor Otto III held in Gniezno in the year 1000. Successive rulers gradually expanded Polish territory, incorporating it into the new Dukedom. However, a period of weakened statehood occurred after the 1138 death of Bolesław Krzywousty ("the Wrymouth"), whose last will assigned authority in each of five different parts of Poland to different Princes – his sons, with the most important deemed to be the one residing in Kraków.

At the end of the 13th century and beginning of the 14th, Władysław Łokietek ("the Short") united the country once again. It was at this time that the power of the Teutonic Order of Knights of St. Mary the Virgin was growing in the north. Władysław the Short's successor, Kazimierz the Great, was nevertheless able to extend Polish territory still further, as well as promoting economic development and the increased significance of Poland in the international arena.

The death of Kazimierz the Great in 1370 brought an end to the rule of the Piast dynasty. On the strength of agreements entered into previously with the Angevins, the throne of Poland was taken up by Louis of Hungary, and after his death in 1384 by Jadwiga. It was her marriage of the same year to Lithuanian King Władysław Jagiełło that started the Jagiellonian Dynasty of the nearly 200-year period 1386-1572.

Under the King's command, the combined armies of Poland and Lithuania were successful in taking on the Teutonic Knights at the Battle of Grunwald in 1410. It was nevertheless to be some time later before the Knights received their final defeat – at the hands of Kazimierz IV Jagiellon, the ultimate victor of the Thirteen Years' War of 1454-1466. Further territory was gained in this way, and it was under the last of the Jagiellons – Zygmunt I "the Old", as well as Zygmunt II August – that Mazowsze (then Masovia) was added to Poland, while a peace agreement with Turkey was signed and the Parliament convened in Lublin in 1569 founded a Union between Poland and Lithuania known as the Commonwealth of the Two Nations. This was a strong state

under one ruler, with a joint Parliament and foreign policy. Unsurprisingly, then, the 16th century is considered to have been a "golden age" for Poland.

However, the death of Zygmunt August with no heir in 1572 ended the rule of the Jagiellons, leaving kingship a matter for elections by the nobility. There was to be no immediate successor to Zygmunt as one candidate for the Polish throne after another tried to win the support of electors by offering ever greater rights and privileges, and simultaneously eroding the rights and strength of the monarchy. The inevitable result

Map of the Commonwealth of the Two Nations

Jan III Sobieski (1624-1696).

"The Election of Stanisław August", by Bernardo Bellotto, alias Canaletto.

as the elected Kings came and went was increasing chaos and enfeebled statehood. Most of the occupants of the throne from them on were not committed to a strengthened Poland, as they were not Poles and had no expectation that their descendants would accede to the throne after them. Moreover, the country was suffering depopulation and economic decline in the 17th century, as epidemics coincided with the onset of a long-lasting conflict with Sweden ultimately resulting in the invasion known as "The Deluge", with wars against Moscow and Turkey as well, and with threats to eastern parts from Cossack uprisings. It was thus in a splendid exception to an otherwise rather miserable rule of those times that Jan III Sobieski came to the throne in 1674. Under him, convincing and crucial victories were won over the Turks at Chocim in 1673 and Vienna ten years later. Sobieski died – in a Poland at peace – in 1696, justifiably proud of his achievements and little suspecting that the approaching 18th century would in the main be an era of decline, as ever greater influence over Poland came to be exerted by its muscle-flexing imperial neighbours in Russia, Prussia and Austria. However, something of a valiant attempt to reverse this trend through renewed Polish statehood came with the 1764 election of King Stanisław August Poniatowski (who would in fact be Poland's last). Doubtless appreciating the threat posed to their authority, the neighbours engaged in the First Partition of Poland in 1772, provoking a patriotic response from the side of King and country, as the Commission on National Education was founded in 1773 and the Four-Year Sejm summoned in 1788. The culmination of this Parliament's activity was a magnificent, if doomed, gesture in the form of the enactment of the Constitution of May 3rd 1791 – the first of its kind in Europe and only the second in the world. The inevitable crackdown followed, with the Second Partition of 1793, followed by the Third and last of 1795 that ended Polish independence and erased the country from the map of Europe. King Stanisław was forced into abdication and exile.

Polish armies arising subsequently – also in exile – played an active part in the wars prosecuted by France, counting on some kind of reward in the shape of Napoleon's support for their country's independence. In the event, the French defeat of the Prussians led to the creation of the Duchy of Warsaw in 1807.

It was sadly to prove ephemeral as, with the French defeat in and retreat from Moscow, the Russian army poured into Warsaw in 1813. Two years later, the Congress of Vienna decided on the creation of a "Congress" Kingdom of Poland entirely subordinated to Russia. A number of uprisings or other forms of resistance against the three different occupying powers were to follow, but the chances were basically zero until all three of the Partitioners found themselves on the losing side of World War I. The newly-independent Poland of 1918 slowly began to make up for more than 100 years deprived of its liberty. But the development of the economy, education, culture and art soon took on ever-greater dynamism, only for hopes to be dashed again so soon, as World War II broke out. Having to face aggression from both its eastern and western neighbours, Poland was probably World War II's greatest victim. The ruins it had been reduced to, and the millions of deaths it had suffered, by 1945, were worse than anything even its troubled history could recall. Worst of all, in the wake of such sacrifice, the status of Poland as one of the ultimately victorious allies (having fought on all fronts throughout) was not even rewarded by full post-War independence. Rather, the Teheran and Yalta Conferences of 1943 and 1945 agreed that Poland would fall "within the Soviet sphere of influence" – something which in fact meant complete submission to communist Moscow. This was a state of affairs that the Poles were to try and resist for years, proving ready to fight on for their democracy, and finally bringing about the 1980 establishment of the Solidarity trade union as a force opposing the communist authorities. Mass Solidarity-led protests from the public led to a state crackdown and the imposition of martial law on December 13th 1981. Only at the "Round Table" talks of 1989 did the authorities meet with representatives of the opposition. This was the death knell for communism, and a steady moved towards democracy followed. Solidarity leaders Lech Wałęsa and Tadeusz Mazowiecki being freely elected President and Prime Minister respectively. The return of national sovereignty led Poland to seek NATO membership, which it achieved on Marh 12th 1999. In turn, economic development and political will allowed the country to accede to the European Union on May 1st 2004.

POLAND'S GEOGRAPHY

Pogorzelica – and its wide, sandy beaches.

Gdynia Orłowo – the coastal cliffs.

Poland is in Central Europe, but is also a Baltic Sea country, with its precise limits being set by meridians 14°07'E and 24°08'E, and parallels 49°00'N and 54°50'N. It covers 312,685 km². The latitudinal extent is sufficient to ensure that summer days on the coast are more than one hour longer than those in the mountains of the far south. The reverse situation applies in winter. Equally, the country extends far enough in the E-W direction to ensure a 40-minute difference in times of sunset and sunrise. Although in the Central European time zone, Eastern European time is adhered to in summer. The climate is temperate, though Poland lies within the transition zone between oceanic and continental influences. As a consequence, the weather is variable from season to season and from year to year. Today's Poland has seven neighbours: Germany to the west, the Czech Republic and Slovakia to the south, Ukraine, Belarus and Lithuania to the east and Russia's Kaliningrad District to the north. There are also 528 km of Baltic shoreline. The country's capital, Warsaw (Warszawa) has 1,700,000 people and is not far from the geometric centre of Europe.

In geomorphological terms, Poland finds itself at the meeting point of three large tectonic units, namely: the Eastern European Pre-Cambrian Platform, the Central and Western European Palaeozoic Platform and the Alpids Orogen (mountain formation). Poland is nevertheless a prevalently lowland country, with more than 91% of its area below 300 m a.s.l., and an average altitude of just 173 m (cf. a European average of 330 m). The lowest point is in the Vistula Delta area near Raczki Elbląskie (at 1.8 m below sea level), while the highest is the 2499 m south-western peak of Mt. Rysy in the High Tatras.

The relief and landscape of the country are thus varied, with the southern mountain belt of varying height, geological structure and age giving way to the north to an extensive upland, then a central plain as flat as a pancake, a series of picturesque lakelands, forests and marshes some way in from the coast and the coastal belt itself. Rivers thus range from fast-flowing mountain brooks to lazily meandering lowland rivers both big and small.

So, the southern border with Slovakia is formed by the Western Carpathians (peaking in the High and Western Tatra ranges). North of this is the Podhale Basin, and beyond it a further range collectively called the Beskids, and including the Western Beskids (as divided into the High and Low ranges), as well as the Eastern Beskids and Bieszczady Mountains, stretching beyond the Łupkowska Pass to the meeting point of the Polish, Slovakian and Ukrainian borders. In general, the Beskids have rounded tops and numerous valleys. Extending to the north of them is the Carpathian Foreland and beyond that (as separated by the Sandomierz and Oświęcim Basins) is a further belt of uplands and old mountains, separated by depressions and called – from west to east – the Silesian Upland, the Małopolska Upland (comprising the Kraków-Częstochowa Upland, Woźniki-Wieluń Upland, the Nida Syncline, the Kielce-Sandomierz Upland and Świętokrzyskie Mountains) and the Lublin Upland and Roztocze. The highest of these ranges are the Świętokrzyskie ("Holy Cross") Mountains, Palaeozoic in origin, with their characteristic upper parts including quartzite screes.

The south west of the country bordering with the Czech Republic also boasts the Sudety range – Poland's second highest mountains. These comprise many sub-ranges, including – on the Polish side – the Kaczawskie and Sowie Mountains, and parts of the Izerskie, Karkonosze, Stołowe, Bystrzyckie and Złote Mountains. The

Siemiany – lakeland.

Karkonosze (peaking at 1602 m Śnieżka) form the highest and best-known range. North of the Sudety there begins the belt of Central Polish Lowlands extending all the way to the eastern border, and contiguous with plains of a similar kind going all the way to the Urals. Included within the Polish part are the Silesian, Wielkopolska, Mazowsze (Mazovian), Podlasie and Polesie-Lublin Plains, with their peaceful rustic landscapes.

North of the plains, and again extending across the whole country and beyond is a lakeland belt. This comprises the Wielkopolska and Pomeranian Lakelands west of the River Vistula, as well as the famous Mazurian Lakeland to the east. The lakes lie in the depressions between relatively high elevations, with the entire landscape having been "bulldozed" into this kind of shape by the ice sheets of the last Ice Age. The Mazurian Lakeland has the greatest number of lakes, and the biggest.

The Baltic Coast in turn features a lowland plain with two particular depressions where the Rivers Odra (Oder) and Wisła (Vistula) meander down to the sea. However, while most of the shore is flat and sandy, with spits, lagoons and dunes, there are stretches of steep and relatively high cliffs, being continually regenerated by the cutting action of the waves below.

99.7% of Poland is within the Baltic Sea basin, with 55.7% being drained by the Vistula (the country's largest river) and 33.9% by the Oder. 9.3% of the country is drained by rivers feeding directly into the Baltic, 0.8% is within the basin of the Neman, while rain falling in just 0.3% of the far south-west or far south-east respectively will ultimately make its way to the Black and North Seas. The river network is diverse - densest in the Carpathian and Sudety Mountains on account of the high rainfall, rather impermeable substratum and diversified relief. Poland has around 9300 lakes covering more than 1 ha, most in the aforementioned lakelands. The deepest lakes are lowland Lake Hańcza (112 m), and Wielki Staw Polski in the Tatras (79.3 m). L. Śniardwy covers the largest area (109.7 km²).

The Polish tradition in the conservation of nature extends back to the Middle Ages. As early as in the 11th century, Bolesław Chrobry ordered restrictions on the trapping of beavers, while Kazimierz the Great (in 1347) and Władysław Jagiełło (in 1423) introduced bans on the cutting of old oaks and yews. In 1868 the Parliament in Lvov issued an act of law – the first of its kind in the world – bringing mountain fauna (chamois and marmots) under protection. The Poland of today boasts no fewer than 23 National Parks, among which 6 feature on the UNESCO world list of Biosphere Reserves. More than 100 Landscape Parks have been established, and in excess of 1000 Nature Reserves. More than 70 different mineral resources are exploited, 40% involves the working of hard coal, 35% sand and gravel, 8% each brown coal and limestone, and the remainder sulphur, rock salt, copper ore, iron ore, zinc, lead, nickel, barite and silver. Also of major economic significance are Poland's granites, marbles and

The Suwałki region – a post-glacial landscape.

Mazowsze – a land of plains.

The foothills of the Silesian Beskids.

The Tatra Mountains and their high-mountain landscape.

sandstones. The country also has a wealth of waters of geothermal value, and hot springs that have favoured spa treatment with waters containing chlorides, bicarbonates and sulphurous compounds.

1 ZACHODNIOPOMORSKIE

VOIVODSHIP (WESTERN POMERANIA)

Capital: **SZCZECIN**

Situated in the north west and taking in a large part of the region known for a century as **Western Pomerania**, it covers almost 30,000 km². To the west lies Germany, to the north the Baltic shore. The area retains traces of the various spheres of influence it has come under down the centuries: of Polish and German rulers, those of Denmark and Brandenburg; in the 17th century it came under Swedish rule, but a hundred years later it was German. Only after the Second World War did this part of Europe come once again within the territorial limits of Poland.

The seat of the voivodship is **Szczecin** – a city with a long and interesting history. The first

walled township appeared here in the 9th century, on the site of an old settlement of the Lusatian culture (dated to 500 B.C.). Szczecin officially became a town in the 13th century, and at the same time a member of the Hanseatic League. From that day to this it has been the main centre of Western Pomerania, and it also retains its strong links with the sea and navigation (as a great port and shipbuilding centre). The most important heritage items here include the **Castle of the Dukes of Pomerania, the Gothic Cathedral** of St. James the Apostle and the **Chrobry Enbankment** from the beginning of the 20th century.

Szczecin, a city on the Szczecin Lagoon and commercial port. Its Old Market Square features colourful restored tenement houses.

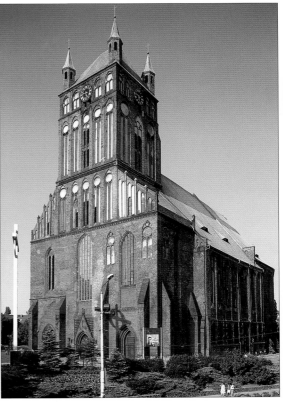

Szczecin. Wały Chrobrego is a leading thoroughfare along the Oder, lined by monumental buildings from the early 20th century.

Szczecin. The Gothic-style Cathedral of St. James the Apostle was rebuilt as recently a in the years 1971-1975, having been destroyed during the Second World War.

The voivodship has other seaports in the form of **Darłowo**, **Świnoujście** and **Kołobrzeg**, and these are the region's largest centres, along with **Koszalin** and **Stargard Szczeciński**. The voivodship is famed for its beautiful coast, its fine nature and its health resorts. A characteristic element along the seashore is constituted by the steep **cliffs** – very high in places and constantly being cut away by the waves. The Baltic claims about 80 cm a year on average, and, although the cliff is reinforced in many places, nature is merciless and has time on her side. If you don't believe it, go and see what is left of the 15th-century **church in Trzęsacz**, once 1800 metres inland – all but one wall has now crashed down

Międzyzdroje, a seaside holiday and health resort

Trzęsacz. Ruins of the 15th-c. Gothic church on a high cliff, washed away by the sea

Dziwnówek, another sunset over the Baltic.

the cliff into the sea beneath.

The region also has **in excess of 1000 lakes**, several tens of rivers and the fine Goleniów, Wkrzańska, Barlinek, Drawsko and Myśliwskie Forests. The two National Parks include that occupying the most interesting, greater part of **Wolin island**. An attraction for the visitor there is the **European Bison Show Reserve**. Drawieński National Park in turn includes **Lake Drawsko** – Poland's second deepest at up to 79.3 m. The bunkers of the **Pomeranian Fortifications** remain in place not far away. Both National Parks feature rare wildlife like

Kamień Pomorski, an old port town with an historic urban layout. The 16th-c. Town Hall

Dziwnów is a large seaside resort, but also a fishing port.

Darłowo. A fountain with fishermen by the Baroque Town Hall.

Forest landscape around **Choszczno**.

Biały Bór. *Zakład Treningowy Koni (the Equestrian Training Centre) is a riding and stud centre.*

white-tailed eagles, ospreys, otters and beavers. Another treat for nature-lovers at migration time are Poland's **largest congregations of cranes**, to be seen near Ińsko.

The best-known holiday resorts in the area are: **Darłowo, Dąbki, Mielno, Sarbinowo, Ustronie Morskie, Dźwirzyno, Mrzeżyno, Niechorze, Rewal** and **Kamień Pomorski**. In turn, at the health resorts like **Świnoujście, Międzyzdroje, Kołobrzeg** and **Połczyn-Zdrój**, you can take a cure in the form of deposits of therapeutic muds and healing spring waters. Many localities retain at least some features of earlier architecture – castles, palaces, and churches, parts of town walls with towers and gates, and old tenement houses. Darłowo features: a **castle of the Dukes of Pomerania** erected between the 14th and 17th centuries,

Połczyn Zdrój, *a holiday and health resort with a fine spa park*

and the Gothic St. Mary's Church dating back to 1394, and often remodelled subsequently. In **Koszalin**, the visitor's attention is drawn to the Gothic-style Church of the Virgin Mary with its imposing tower. Inside it plays host to many valuable works of art. Move east of Koszalin and **Krąg** is seen to contain a rather unusual castle with 4 towers, 12 entrances, 52 rooms and 365 windows. **Biały Bór** in turn retains innocent-looking tenement houses that are actually the upper parts of huge bunkers. Other interesting monuments can be seen in **Białogard**, **Trzebiatów** (the palace complex), **Gryfice**, **Kamień Pomorski**, **Płoty**, **Nowogard**, **Stargard**, **Świdwin**, **Tuczno** and **Połczyn-Zdrój**.

*At **Korytowo**, the church is in the Late Gothic style.*

Stargard Szczeciński. *The Pyrzycka Gate is part of the city's defensive walls.*

POMORSKIE (POMERANIA)
VOIVODSHIP

Capital: **GDAŃSK**

This 18,000 km² part of Pomerania, sometimes termed **Gdańsk Pomerania**, was within Poland up to the 12th century, before becoming an independent dukedom until the 14th century, when it was taken by the Teutonic Knights. The second half of the 15th century brought a return to Poland maintained to the time of the Partitions, when the area passed to Prussia. In 1919 it became Polish again, though Gdańsk itself retained **Free City** status (as Danzig). At 4.45 on September 1st 1939, the German bombardment of the nearby Westerplatte peninsula launched World War II. Apart from Westerplatte, the most eagerly-visited attraction in the Gdańsk area is the city's Main Town full of charming corners, and featuring fine churches, decorative tenement houses and museums. The Church of The Blessed Virgin Mary, **Poland's largest**, holds precious works of art, including a copy of Hans Memling's **"Last Judgment"** and a Gothic sculpture of the Beautiful Madonna. Equally interesting is the Main Town's Gothic-style **Town Hall** with its 82 m tower and exquisite interiors. Catching the eye in the port area on the Motława is the **Old Crane** once serving to load and unload goods,

Gdańsk is a historic port city once within the Hanseatic League. Here the Gothic Town Hall of the Main Town seen on the Long Market.

Gdańsk. The interior of the Gothic-style St. Mary's Church is severe, but many priceless works of art – including an original font – are to be found here.

Gdańsk. *The Neptune Fountain on Długi Targ (the Long Market).*

Gdynia, is a large commercial, naval and passenger port. The World War II naval vessel the "Błyskawica" is moored by the southern quay.

Gdańsk, Westerplatte – a monument to those who fell at the very start of the Second World War was erected here in 1945.

Sopot. The Grand Hotel built in the years 1924-7 is right by the beach.

and one of the largest of its kind in Mediaeval Europe.

Gdańsk is joined by Sopot and Gdynia in creating what is known as the Trójmiasto (**"Tri-City"**) – an urban complex covering 415 km² in all. Gdynia is one the country's youngest cities, becoming the most modern and largest Baltic port just prior to WWII. Floating museums worth a visit include the **"Dar Pomorza" sailing ship** and the **Polish Navy's "Błyskawica"**. Sopot, in turn, was a flourishing, elegant and fashionable spa in the late 19th and early 20th centuries, with the presence of casinos and horse racing going some way to justifying its nickname

Jastarnia. A summer resort on the spit known as the Hel Peninsula.

Słowiński National Park, by the Baltic shore, was founded in 1967. Its mobile dunes are its biggest attraction.

as the "Northern Riviera". It still boasts **Europe's longest wooden pier**, as well as the **Forest Opera** that plays host each year to the city's International Song Festival.

The largest centre in the western part of the voivodship is **Słupsk**, whose monuments to past history include the castle of the Dukes of Pomerania, parts of the defensive walls, the city gates, a castle mill, churches and tenement houses.

One of the most precious monuments of defensive architecture, entered on UNESCO's World Heritage List, is the **Castle in Malbork**, the **former capital of the Teutonic Knights**. Also dating back to this era are the castles in **Gniew**, **Bytów**, **Kwidzyn** and **Człuchów**. Of particular note is the former Cistercian Monastery complex in **Pelplin**, which dates back

Pelplin. The Cathedral of the Blessed Virgin Mary is part of an old Cistercian Abbey complex.

Kartuzy. The interior of the Gothic-Baroque Church of the Assumption is of stone and brick.

to the 13th and 14th centuries. Among the elements characterizing the Gothic appearance restored in the 19th century are interesting Gothic and Renaissance style stalls, as well as fine frescoes in the cloisters.

Pomerania pleases tourists with its beautiful beaches, plentiful lakes and forests. There are two National Parks – Słowiński in the north, renowned for its **mobile dunes** up to 30 m high and the Bory Tucholskie (Tuchola Forest) NP in the south.

The Pomeranian part of the Baltic coast resembles the Western Pomeranian in being varied. There are both cliffs and wide, sandy

Chojnice is a town on the edge of the Tuchola Forest. The market square features this Neo-Gothic Town Hall.

Malbork. The castle, which was the seat of the Teutonic Order's Grand Masters, dates back to the 13th-15th centuries, and is one of the finest surviving examples of a Mediaeval fortress.

Kwidzyn has a brick-built Gothic cathedral complex devoted to the Virgin Mary and St. John the Envangelist, as well as a castle with square courtyard.

Gniew. Overlooking the Vistula is a 14th-century castle of the Teutonic Knights that was built in the shape of a regular square.

beaches, as well as dunes, forests, spits and lagoon-lakes behind sandbars (like **Łebsko**, **Gardno** and **Sarbsko**). The most popular coastal resorts are **Ustka**, **Rowy**, **Łeba**, **Jastrzębia Góra**, Władysławowo and **Puck**, as well as **Jastarnia** and **Krynica Morska** sited on the Hel and Vistula Spits respectively. Inland, tourists seek rest and recreation around the lakes in **Charzykowo**, **Chmielno**, **Przywidz** and **Wdzydze Kiszewskie**, or else obtain a closer look on canoe trips.

Człuchów. Relics of the Gothic castle of the Teutonic Knights include this octagonal brick tower.

3 KUJAWSKO-POMORSKIE
VOIVODSHIP (KUJAWY-POMERANIA)

Capital: **BYDGOSZCZ**

This voivodship takes in the **Kujawy** region itself (historically Kuyavia), and part of Pomerania, as well as the Dobrzyń land and areas historically associated with Wielkopolska. The capital is **Bydgoszcz** on the Rivers Brda and Vistula. Its development, beginning from the 14th century, was based mainly on the salt and cereal trades. The best-known buildings are the Late Gothic Church in the Old Town and the three old **grain stores by the Brda**. An equally important city in the province is **Toruń**, which is entered on UNESCO's World Heritage List on account of its **preserved Mediaeval town plan in the Old Town** area, as well as its several hundred heritage buildings, principally in the Gothic and Baroque styles (the Town Hall, churches, the castle of the Teutonic Knights, the Crooked Tower and tenement houses). The house in which **Nicholas Copernicus** was born now has a museum devoted to this great astronomer. It is also worth remembering the famous **Toruń gingerbread**, baked in a host of different shapes...

A further city of importance in the voivodship is **Włocławek**, which is renowned for the beautiful ceramics produced there. **Grudziądz**, in turn, also retains a Mediaeval town plan and monuments of its own – above all a complex

Bydgoszcz. *The Market Square features tenement houses of styles ranging from the Baroque, through the Neo-Classical, to the Secessionist and Modernist.*

Bydgoszcz. *The so-called Bydgoszcz Venice comprises old buildings on the River Brda.*

Bydgoszcz, *with the Statue of the Archer.*

of 26 granaries erected between the 14th and 17th centuries on the escarpment above the Vistula. Also noteworthy here is the Gothic church and fragments of the 14th-century city walls. The best-preserved and known **castle** in this area is the one in **Golub-Dobrzyń**. **Knight tournaments** of international rank take place here, and the castle of the Teutonic Knights in the village of Zamek Bierzgłowski remains in a fairly good state. In contrast, in Radzyń Chełmiński, **Świecie** and **Wenecja** the castles have been reduced to ruins. In **Kruszwica**, there is a **tower** known as **Mysia**, in which a legendary King Popiel is said to have been

Koronowo. *The ornate Baroque fittings of the Gothic Church of the Assumption forming part of the former Cistercian complex.*

eaten by mice, thereby leaving the throne available for the Piast dynasty. Beautiful heritage architecture can also be seen in **Lubostroń, Jabłonów Pomorski, Brodnica, Chełmno** (sourrounded still by its old defensive walls), **Mogilno, Skępe, Strzelno** (with its **Romanesque rotunda** of St. Procopius), **Chełmża, Włocławek** and many other places. **Biskupin** is a worth a visit, boasting a **reconstruction of a pre-Slavic settlement**

Biskupin. A reconstruction of the pre-Slavic settlement with defensive ramparts and houses.

from the Halstadtian period (550-400 B.C.). The site hosts **archaeological festivals** at which the visitor may really see how every day life in those far off times must have looked. Many other places in the voivodship give testimony to the very early settlement of the area: the village of **Wietrzychowice** has megalithic burial grounds 4000 years old, while the oldest exhibits at the museum in Kruszwica data back more than 4500 years. Other kinds of interesting collections are held by other museums: ethnographic items and ceramics in Włocławek, the **pictures of Leon Wyczółkowski** in Bydgoszcz, and railway items at the **Museum of the Narrow-Gauge Railway** in Wenecja.

Natural resources of the Kujawy area include its

Wenecja. Old steam engines at the Museum of Narrow-Gauge Railways.

Mogilno. The Church of St. John the Evangelist is Romanesque-Gothic in style, with a two-tower Baroque façade in what was once a Benedictine Abbey.

deposits of salt. Research has shown that this was already being worked two centuries B.C. At **Ciechocinek** and **Inowrocław**, salty waters have been used as **spa cures** – for respiratory complaints among other things – for more than 150 years. The wooden structures wherein such waters are converted into fine sprays and inhaled are from the 19th century and the complex is **the biggest of its kind in the world**. The most popular holiday centres in this region are **Koronowo**, **Brodnica**, **Tuchola**, **Bachotek**, the **Chełmża** area, **Kruszwica** and **Biskupin**. There are Landscape Parks and a number

Strzelno. Built from granite blocks is the Romanesque Church of St. Procopius.

Kruszwica. A hangover from the days of the 14th-century castle is the eight-sided Mysia Wieża, from which views of Lake Gopło can be enjoyed.

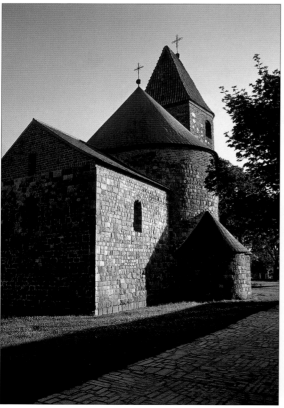

*Sunset over **Lake Sumińskie** in the Dobrzyń Lakeland.*

__Golub-Dobrzyń__ boasts a 14th-century castle remodelled in Renaissance style in the 1600s. Each year, this plays host to tournaments of jousting and other chivalrous skills.

of nature reserves, as well as several massive oaks: one in Nogat has a trunk of circumference 940 cm, while another in Bąkowo has almost as great a girth, of 890 cm. In turn, within the Tuchola Forest, near Osłuchowo, stands another monument of nature, St. Adalbert's Stone. This **glacial erratic** (boulder carried by ice sheets and dropped when they melted) has a circumference of 24.5 m and a height of 3.5 m.

__Brodnica__. A heritage-rich small town on the edge of the Brodnica Lakeland, which features such buildings as these restored 18th-19th century tenement houses.

4 WARMIŃSKO-MAZURSKIE
VOIVODSHIP (WARMIA-MAZURY)

Capital: **OLSZTYN**

The voivodship includes two picturesque lands from history, i.e. **Varmia** and **Mazuria**. It is known even more colourfully as the "Land of the Thousand Lakes" and has only around 1.5 million people across its 24,000 km². Varmia was originally inhabited by a Prussian tribe of a similar name, as one of the Balt peoples settled from the middle of the first millennium A.D. in the land between the mouths of the Vistula and Neman. Later, and particularly during the region's **occupation by the Teutonic Knights**, the people became Germanised and annihilated. Mazuria also belonged to the Prussians in the early Middle Ages, though it was colonized by Poles from neighbouring Mazovia from the 14th century on. Today's Varmia-Mazury is **home to many cultures** – the core population of inhabitants whose ancestors settled here long ago, plus those of Polish and Ukrainian origin, Lemko people and the descendents of Germans. There are Catholics and Evangelical Protestants, as well as followers of the Byzantine-Ukrainian church.

The voivodship capital is **Olsztyn**, a city founded in the 14th century by the Teutonic Knights. It was Polish from 1446 to 1772, then Prussian

Olsztyn. Freedom Square (Plac Wolności) with its early 20th-century Town Hall built in a style that recalls the Baroque and Renaissance periods.

Olsztyn on the River Łyna and within the Olsztyn Lakeland. This reconstructed 14th-century castle was that of the Varmia Chapter.

Miłomłyn, and Lake Ruda Woda, which
has the Elbląg Canal flowing through it.

Morąg. The 16th-century palace
of the Dohn family was rebuilt at the
beginning of the 18th century.

under the Partitions, then Polish once again post
1945. **Copernicus** spent several years of his life
here, being administrator of the Varmia Chapter
and preparing the place for defence against the
Teutonic Knights. The astronomer lives in the
castle of the aforementioned chapter which
still stands today as the present seat of the
Museum of Varmia and Mazury.

The second most important city in the region is
Elbląg, which obtained its charter as early as in
the 13th century, at which time it was the seat
of the Teutonic Knights and a member of the
Hanseatic League. It had a large port, and
Poland's first shipyard from 1570 onwards.

Lubawa. The Gothic St. Anne's Church
with its characteristic front tower.

Iława on Lake Jeziorak. The Gothic Church of the Transfiguration.

Grunwald. Knights of today fight on the site of the famous victory over the Teutonic Knights of 1410.

The partition of 1772 left it in Prussian hands, and it did not return to Poland until after World War II.

The voivodship's many heritage buildings include the **fortified cathedral in Frombork**, the **collegiate church in Dobre Miasto**, the **castles built by the Teutonic Knights in Kętrzyn, Nidzica and Ostróda**, the castle of the Bishops of Varmia in Reszel, the Bishops' castles in **Szymbark** and **Lidzbark Warmiński**, and the churches in **Święta Lipka, Braniewo, Elbląg, Olsztyn** and **Kętrzyn**. At **Grunwald**, the **1410 victory of Poland** over the Teutonic

Grunwald. Visible from afar on its mound is the Monument to the Victory and Grunwald.

Lidzbark Welski. *The shores of Lake Lidzbarskie have holiday centres and camping sites.*

Barczewo. *The Gothic Town Hall, remodelled in the 19th c.*

Kętrzyn *is an old Prussian settlement that was later a stronghold of the Teutonic Knights. St. George's Church is brick-built in the Gothic style.*

Mrągowo *is a town famous for its annual "Piknik Country" festival.*

Szczytno. *View over Lake Długie of the former Gothic castle of the Teutonic Knights.*

Lidzbark Warmiński. *Part of the castle of the Bishops of Varmia, built of brick in the Gothic style.*

Knights that happened here is commemorated at a Monument to the event. A further major attraction of the region is the 19th-century **Elbląg Canal**, with its locks, inclines and aqueduct passing over the surface of a lake. In turn, the region's forests retain ruins of **German bunkers from World War II**: the most famous of all, **Hitler's former HQ** near Gierłoż, as well as the **Wehrmacht headquarters** in Mamerki, and Gołdap and Pozedrze. Varmia-Mazury is above all a tourist region. Apart from in Olsztyn and Elbląg there is no heavy industry to speak of here, and so this is the cleanest part of Poland. It boasts several Landscape Parks and a great many Nature Reserves, in which rare species of fauna and flora enjoy protection. It is also the perfect place for **tourism based around water**, with the shores

Święta Lipka *boasts a Baroque Jesuit monastery complex with the Church of the Visitation. The interior of the latter has a famous organ with moving decorative elements.*

of lakes boasting many jetties, harbours and watersports centres (including those for winter sports). Trips by canoe and passenger cruises are organized, while the forests on the lakeshores support holiday centres and camping sites. The greatest numbers of tourists choose to holiday around **Giżycko**, **Mikołajki**, **Ruciane-Nida**, **Mrągowo**, **Morąg**, **Iława**, **Gołdap**, **Olsztyn**, **Olsztynek** and **Ostróda**.

*The **Borecka Forest** is a large forest complex in the Ełk Lakeland.*

5 PODLASKIE
VOIVODSHIP (PODLASIE)

Capital: **BIAŁYSTOK**

Situated in the north-eastern corner of Poland, this voivodship includes the **Suwałki region** and part of what was historically **Podlasie**. It borders to the east with Lithuania and Belarus, and retains several different cultures – of **Poles**, **Byelorussians**, **Lithuanians**, and the **descendents of Tartars** settling in several villages here as long ago as in the times of Jan III Sobieski. To this day, Catholics, Orthodox worshippers and Moslems live side by side in this region. Different borders have also passed through it at different times, e.g. between Poland and the Grand Duchy of Lithuania, between the Prussian and Russian parts of partitioned Poland and later between Prussia and the Congress Kingdom. Most of the land here came back to Poland in 1918.

Larger urban agglomerations are simply not to be found here. The closest the region can come is with its capital of **Białystok**, with 280,000 people. This was devastated during the Second World War, though some reconstructed buildings include the Town Hall, which is now the seat of the District Museum. But the city's most important building is the **Branicki Palace** and surrounding park housing the headquarters of the School of Medicine. Other more important towns in the region include **Łomża**,

Białystok. *The interior of the Baroque place of the Branicki family. The Medical Scool's "Aula Magna" brasts rich stucco-work, paintings and tapestries.*

Białystok, on the River Biała, was founded in the 15th century. The Baroque palace and park complex of the Branicki family has won it self the nickname "the Versailles of Podlasie"

Białystok. A post-War reconstruction is the Baroque Town Hall now housing the District Museum.

Wasilków. The 19th-century Orthodox Church in the Neo-Classical/Byzantine style.

Suwałki, Augustów, Wysokie Mazowieckie
and Grajewo.

Podlasie voivodship is a little-industrialised part of the country, with a wealth of **unspoilt nature**, wild forests and unregulated rivers (like the world-famous **Biebrza**). In terms of the purity of its air, this is Poland's second cleanest voivodship (after Varmia-Mazury). Much of it is covered in forest, and this sometimes forms large complexes of a primaeval character. Examples here are the world-famous Białowieża Forest, as well as those in the Augustów and Knyszyn areas, and the so-called Czerwony Bór ("Red Forest").

Sokółka, once a forest settlement of the Lithuanian dukes. The Neo-classical parish church.

The **Tykocin** museum. A gallery of Zygmunt Bujanowski 's paintings in a 19th-20th century parlour setting.

Tykocin. The interior of the Baroque synagogue is now a museum to Judaism.

The Suwałki Region. Post-glacial erratics are a characteristic element of the landscape.

Unsurprisingly then, no less than 40% of the province enjoys legal protection and there are four **National Parks**: Białowieski (containing the aforementioned Białowieża Forest), Narwiański along the River Narew, Biebrzański along the Biebrza and Wigierski around the large Lake Wigry. These areas are augmented by the Suwałki, Łomża, Bug River and Knyszyn Forest Landscape Parks and more than 800 Nature Reserves. Beavers, wolves, lynxes and **European bison** can all be found here, the latter **the pride of the region** and whole country.

A Lock at Przewięź on the **Augustów Canal**, between Lakes Białe and Studziennicze.

Stańczyki. A viaduct of an old (never-finished) railway, which claims the record as Poland's highest.

Wigry. The formerly Calmeldolite monastery complex with its Baroque-style Church of the Immaculate Conception, situated by Lake Wigry.

The **River Jerzgnia** in Woźnawieś near Rajgród.

The 300 lakes in the region include **Hańcza**, Poland's deepest. **Navigation** is rather well developed, and the conditions are fine for waterborne tourism, especially by canoe. A **waterway** of heritage significance is the **Augustów Canal** dating back to the first half of the 19th century and linking the Vistula and Neman Basins. The Canal is 102 km long, has 18 stone locks and can carry vessels of up to 100 tonnes.

A good break away from it all can be taken in **Augustów** itself, by L. Wigry, or in the **Suwałki** and **Siemianówka** areas. There are plenty

Ciechanowiec. The display of old steam-powered machinery at the open-air museum

The Biebrza Marshes in **Biebrzański National Park**
– a natural area unique in Europe.

of architecturally-valuable structures to take in too, notably: **the manor of the Lutosławski family in Drozdowo**, the church and monastery complex by Lake Wigry, and the churches in **Sejny**, **Drohiczyn** and **Siemiatycze**. The region

Grajewo *– The 19th c. church and belfry.*

Nowogród. *The Outdoor Museum of the Kurpie Region.*

Bielsk Podlaski. *The late Baroque Taum Hall on the Market Square.*

Łomża *had town rights from the 14th century onwards – here a tenement house from the late 19th and early 20th centuries holds courtrooms.*

Wysokie Mazowieckie. *The Shrine to the Virgin Mary at the John the Baptist Church.*

Zuzela, *the brithpalce of cardinal Stefan Wyszyński, Primate of Poland till 1981. A classroom in the former school.*

includes a number of churches and sacred sites for the Russian Orthodox Church, e.g. large numbers of churches in places such as **Bielsk Podlaski**, **Białowieża**, **Mielnik**, **Sokółka**, **Białystok** and **Hajnówka**, as well as the **Święta Góra Grabarka** site, with its forest of crosses of penitence brought here by the faithful. Those following the old ritual have their places of worship, known as molenny in **Wodziłki** and **Gabowe Grądy**. Moslems continue to pray at the mosques in **Kruszyniany** and **Bohoniki**; with the former also boasting a **Moslem cemetery**. It is also worth remembering about the museum of Judaism in the old synagogue in Tykocin, the museums of natural history in Białowieża and Drozdowo, and the **open-air museums** in **Ciechanowiec**, **Nowogród** and **Jurowce**.

Białowieża. The European bison
– the biggest tourist attraction.

The global significance of **Białowieża National Park** is reflected in its status as a Biosphere Reserve.

6 MAZOWIECKIE
VOIVODSHIP (MAZOWSZE)

Capital: **WARSZAWA**

Covering 35,000 km², Mazowsze is the **largest** of the voivodships. It also has the **largest population** – in excess of 5 million. Most of it coincides with the historical **Mazowsze** (formerly known as Mazovia or Masovia), which was already within Poland by the period of the 10th – 12th centuries. It was in an independent dukedom for a long time subsequently, however, though it was reincorporated into Poland bit by bit so that all was back within the fold by the first half of the 16th century (following the death of the last Duke of Mazovia without issue). **Warsaw** has been the region's **capital** since the early 17th century.
The partitions saw Mazowsze carved up between the Prussian and Austrians, though at the time of the Napoleonic Wars (1807-1815) it became the Duchy of Warsaw under the French, as it were, and then with their defeat at the hands of the Russians the Congress Kingdom of Poland, little more than a vassal of Moscow. And this is what it stayed until Poland came back on to the map of Europe at the end of World War I. Warsaw is the largest centre of the voivodship in terms of industry, culture and tourism. This was a market and defensive township as early as in the 10th century, but only officially a town from

Warsaw's Castle Square, with the Column of King Zygmunt III Waza in the foreground.

Warsaw. The Old Town Market Square with the Mermaid Statue.

41

Warsaw. These leatherbound volumes form
part of the National Library collection
in the Krasiński Palace.

Warsaw. A portrait of King Stanisław August
Poniatowski by Marcello Bacciarelli in the Royal
Castle's Marble Room.

Warsaw. The Łazienki Park and Palace complex with
its neo-Classical Palace on the Island. This was the
seat of Poland's last King, Stanisław August Poniatowski,
who reigned until 1795.

the mid 13th on. It was the seat of the **Dukes
of Mazovia**, and then – in the 15th century
– the place at which the **Polish-Lithuanian
parliaments** were convened and the **Kings
elected**. Nevertheless, it only became a **royal
place of residence** – and hence the capital
of Poland – in the late 16th and early 17th
centuries. As the years passed, Warsaw flourished
at times, then crashed at others. The Swedish

Warsaw. Wilanów, one of Poland's finest palatial residences,
built for the summer use of King Jan III Sobieski.
Here the front elevation of the 17th-century palace.

Warsaw. In Łazienki Park, the authentic 18th-century interiors of the theatre in the Old Orangery Building have illusionist painting on the ceiling and cornices.

invasion, the Partitions and of course especially the two World Wars were terribly hard on the city. Indeed, the Nazis reduced left-bank Warsaw to **rubble** – almost literally. Thus, just about everything one sees in today's Warsaw centre (including the parts that appear to be centuries old) were rebuilt in the late 1940s onward. Only in the right-bank part of Warsaw (known as Praga) is there any significant amount of pre-War construction still in existence. Thus, Warsaw's must-see Old Town is not old at all, but is nevertheless a World Heritage Site as an example of faithful reconstruction from its pre-War state, in many cases down to the finest detail, and with the surviving original fragments

Warsaw. The controversial Socialist-Realist architecture of the Palace of Culture and Science appeared on the skyline in the years 1952-55. Including the topmost aerial, it rises to 234 m.

Kobyłka. Polychromy in the side aisle of the Late-Baroque Holy Trinity Church.

reincorporated into the structure. The **Royal Castle** is in a similar situation, looking exactly as it did centuries ago, but having been started in the 1970s. The **Wilanów** Park and Palace is another attractive complex to visit, this time on the outskirts of Warsaw at the end of the so-called **Royal Route** that passes all the way from the Old Town, and takes in the exquisite **Łazienki Park**, with its several (also mainly rebuilt) palaces en route. All told, the Trakt Królewski as it is known takes in the Krakowskie Przedmieście, Nowy Świat and Aleje Ujazdowskie thoroughfares, all attractive and worth a stroll, with their many churches, palaces and stylish tenement houses. A quite different scene is that of the city centre proper, dominated as it is by

Zielonka, not far from Warsaw and the picturesque Horowe Marsh.

The **Zegrze Reservoir**, formed by the damming of the Narew, is a place for Varsovians to unwind at weekends.

Sierpc. The Outdoor Museum features
the folk architecture of northern Mazowsze.

Pułtusk on the Narew, former seat of the Bishops of Płock. The
Town Hall in the market square with the 16thc. tower and the
Bishops' Palace, now Polonia House, in the background.

Płock, one of Mazowsze's oldest settlements, dates back
to the 8th century. Its Neo-Classical Town Hall from
the early 19th century has an octagonal tower.

Łyse is a centre of Kurpie-region folk culture
known for its "longest palm" contest on Palm Sunday.

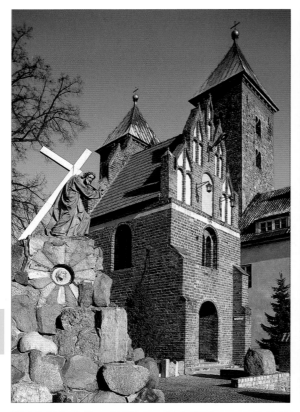

Żelazowa Wola. *The Neo-Classical manor house is the Fryderyk Chopin Museum.*

Czerwińsk *was once a centre of trade along the Vistula.It features a monastery of canons-regular with a Romanesque church.*

Sanniki, *A neo-Renaissance palace stylised as an Italian villa. A statue of Fryderyk Chopin stands in front of it.*

Żyrardów. *The Art Nouveau palace, now the Regional Museum.*

Radziejowice. *The Neo-Gothic castle is linked via a gallery with the Baroque/Neo-Classical palace.*

Ojrzanów. The Neo-Renaissance manor set in fine parkland.

Czersk. The ruins of the 14th-15th century castle, as destroyed by the Swedes, and then the Siedmiogród army.

the imposingly stark **Socialist-Realist architecture of the Palace of Culture and Science**. An example of the Mazovian Gothic style is provided by the impressive ruins of the castle in **Czersk**, as well as the brick-built fortress of the Dukes of Mazovia in **Ciechanów**. The most beautifully-sited town is **Pułtusk**, whose centre is on an island created by the River Narew. Here we find one of the **longest market squares in Europe**, the castle of the Bishops of Płock and the Gothic-Renaissance collegiate church. In **Żelazowa Wola, birthplace of Chopin**, the country manor house holds a museum devoted to the great composer, and **summer concerts** of his music are often organised. The manor in **Czarnolas** is in turn

Stara Błotnica. The miraculous picture of the Consolation Mother of God in this Sanctuary of the Radom region.

Maciejowice. Scythes to the attack – a Monument to Tadeusz Kościuszko as leader of the national rising.

the place of birth and residence of **Jan Kochanowski**, a poet of the Renaissance whose life and works are celebrated in the museum established here.

But Mazowsze is not only cities and museums, as there is also nature to be enjoyed. The characteristic landscape is of extensive plains with rows of **pollarded willows along roads and tracks**. However, a touch of wilderness is also present – on the very limits of Warsaw – in the Kampinos National Park, with its moose, beavers, lynxes, black storks, cranes and eagles. A quite different site also not far from the capital is the Zegrze Reservoir, where rest and recreation can be had in the many holiday centres, and a sail or trip by passenger ferry enjoyed.

Chlewiska: its 19th-century steelworks complex is today the Museum of Technology.

Mazowsze. Stork nests give the landscape
its unique character.

Liw. The remains of the castle of the Dukes
of Mazovia, where the keep and 18th century
manor hold the Museum of Arms and Armour.

At **Stara Wieś**, the mid 19th-century English-Gothic-style
palace stands in picturesque parkland.

Andrzejewo. An interesting coffered ceiling
in the Gothic-style church.

Siedlce. The octagonal Neo-Classical Holy Cross Chapel
was once the chapel of the Ogiński family palace.

7 ŁÓDZKIE (ŁÓDŹ)
VOIVODSHIP

Capital: ŁÓDŹ

Łódź voivodship is in central Poland, comprising part of historical Mazovia plus the Sieradz and Łęczyca areas. The history of most of the area resembles that of Mazovia.

The capital and main industrial district is **the city of Łódź**, which obtained its town rights in the 15th century, but was in the hands of the Bishopric of Włocławek until 1798. The first **cotton mills and weaving mills** appeared there at the beginning of the 19th century. It was not long before the liberal customs regulations regarding trade with Russia – and the unlimited export of textiles to that country this allowed – provoked major growth in the

textile industry. This was to ensure that the city had **the world's biggest textile factories** by the end of the 19th century. Łódź became a cosmopolitan city, with only half of the 600,000-strong population in the inter-War period being Polish (the remainder largely Jewish and German). Immediately after the War, only 250,000 inhabitants were left.

A particularly characteristic feature of Łódź are its **factory complexes** (the owner's mansion plus factory and residential blocks for workers). There are also quite a few tenement houses in the **Secessionist and Eclectic styles**, especially along **Piotrkowska Street**, regarded

*In **Łódź**, the Herbst Palace stands in the Księży Młyn factory estate.*

*The Scheibler Mansion in **Łódź**. This Neo-Classical/Neo-Renaissance palace has not only stylish rooms, but also a Museum of Cinematography.*

Łódź. This Neo-Baroque palace with rich Eclectic facade also has a complex of old spinning mills which belonged to industrialist Izrael Poznański at the end of the 19th century.

as **one of Europe's longest commercial thoroughfares**. The old factory of Ludwig Geyer today houses the Museum of the Textile Industry, with its very rich and interesting collections, while the reconstructed Herbst Mansion is a museum of 19th century interiors from the big houses of the Łódź industrialists. A good example of preserved 19th-century architecture is the weaving-mill complex, together with the magnificent **mansion of magnate Izrael Poznański**. Łódź is also the **city of Polish cinematography**, with the film and theatre school being located here. It was in the interestingly outfitted Scheibler Palace that

Łódź's Poznański Palace – one of the interiors retaining its original decor.

Arkadia, the romantic landscape park.

Walewice has a Neo-Classical palace associated with Maria Walewska, famed for her romance with Napoleon.

Nieborów. Set in extensive parkland, the 17th-century Baroque palace is one of the most valuable heritage buildings in the Mazowsze region.

Oporów. Chivalrous interiors of the oft-rebuilt castle now house museum exhibits.

scenes from the epic "The Promised Land" were filmed. The Museum of Cinematography is housed here today.

One of the voivodship's more interesting attractions is **Arkadia** – a **Romantic-style landscaped park** laid out in the 18th-19th centuries. It boasts a lake with two islands and interesting vegetation, as well as Neo-Gothic and Neo-Classical park buildings scattered around it. The Park was laid out by the landowner in nearby **Nieborów**, where a fine Baroque palace

Uniejów. The remodelled castle dating back to the 14th century was once the residence of Bishops.

Złaków Kościelny. The colourful Corpus Christi procession with its folk costumes.

of beautiful interiors set in parkland boasts a wealth of artwork. Other palaces are to be visited in **Walewice**, **Poddębice**, **Białaczów**, **Wolbórz** (the Palaces of the Bishops of Kujawy), **Pabianice** and **Skierniewice**.
The region's several castles include those: of the Dukes of Mazovia in **Rawa Mazowiecka**, of the Archbishops of Gniezno in **Uniejów** and of King Kazimierz the Great in **Łęczyca**. There is also a 14th-century Gothic castle in **Oporów**, as well as impressive ruins of a Gothic-Renaissance castle at **Drzewica**. In turn, among the many old churches, the most noteworthy are the **Romanesque collegiate church** in **Tum**, as well as the priceless **wooden church** in

Spicimierz not far from Uniejów. On Corpus Christi day, the processional route is strewn with flowers creating a colourful carpet.

Sieradz. Members of the Sieradzanie folk ensemble sport their regional dress.

Boguszyce, the monastery and church in Paradyż, the fortified Cistercian monastery complex in Sulejów, and the churches in **Gidle**, **Łask** and **Inowłódz**.

Łódź voivodship also includes the **Łowicz** and **Opoczno** area, **renowned for its rich folk traditions, including in apparel**. The ladies' folk costume here is considered one of Poland's most beautiful. **Lipce Reymontowskie** in turn has a museum to Władysław Reymont, with a biographical exhibition devoted to the Nobel-prizewinning writer, as well as ethnographic collections. Finally, a fine **dendrological park** and **alpinarium** can be enjoyed at **Rogów**.

Łęczyca marks the place where the devil Boruta once apparently reigned.

A village in the *Sieradz area* with an old thatched hut.

Popowice. A 16th c. wooden church with shingle roof.

Wieluń. *The single-storey Neo-Classical style Town Hall with the Kraków Gate tower merged with the outline of the building.*

Piotrków Trybunalski. *A town since 1313, Piotrków was the 16th-18th century seat of the Crown Tribunal. Here the view of the Baroque Evangelical Church from Trybunalski Square.*

Wielgomłyny – *the Baroque interiors of St. Stanisław's Church in what was once a Paulite monastery complex.*

Sulejów – *one of the best-preserved fortified Cistercian monasteries in Europe.*

In **Ożarów**, *a single-storey timber-built manor house from 1757 is the seat of the Museum of Manorial Interiors.*

8 WIELKOPOLSKIE
VOIVODSHIP (GREATER POLAND)

Capital: **POZNAŃ**

Poland's second largest voivodship, it takes in most of historical **Wielkopolska** (Greater Poland), which is considered the **cradle of the country's statehood**. It was from here that the first dynasty of Polish rulers, the Piast family, came. Among their number was Duke Mieszko I, who based himself in **Gnieźno**, and thus gave Poland **its first capital**. Today the townscape there is dominated by the **Cathedral Basilica** containing one of Europe's finest examples of Romanesque art in the form of the 12th century **bronze doors**. Relics of **St. Adalbert** are also to be seen here in a silver casket, along with a

Gothic-style crucifix from the 15th century and other valuable works of art.

When the Kings of Poland decamped to the new capital, Kraków, Gniezno declined in significance, leaving **Poznań** to take on the role of Wielkopolska's leading city. It had also once been a city of Kings, being a defensive settlement from the 9th century on, as well as the country's first Bishopric from 968 A.D. The oldest part in existence to day is on **Ostrów Tumski** island, where the 14th century Cathedral of Sts. Peter and Paul stands in the place of the aforementioned 9th century

__Poznań__. The Old Market Square with its interestingly arcaded Town Hall.

__Poznań__. Standing in the oldest part of the town is the monumental Cathedral of Sts. Peter and Paul.

Rogalin. This small village on the Warta boasts a Rococo/Neo-Classical style palace in whose design both Domenico Merlini and Jan Christian Kamsetzer had a hand.

fortifications. The **remains of Poland's first rulers**, Mieszko I and Bolesław Chrobry ("the Brave") lie here. The many other fine old buildings include those of the Old Town – dating from the mid 13th century, the castle on Przemysław's Hill, the Neo-Classical Raczyński Library (whose façade is modelled on that of the Louvre) and a host of churches and palaces. The regular Market Square includes the Renaissance **Town Hall** with characteristic arcaded façade and ornate **billy-goats** which battle daily on the stroke of 12 midday. Poznań is a **famed commercial centre**, with its famous Fairs marking a tradition established in the Middle Ages. The first modern fairs were the national

Kórnik. The original castle was extensively remodelled in the English neo-Gothic style in the 19th century.

Golejewko. The 19th-century palace in its landscaped park.

events from 1921 and the **International Fairs** from 1925.

It needs to be recalled that this was not always a Polish centre. The Partitions left the city in Prussian hands, and the new masters' restrictive

Gostyń, with its Philippinian monastery complex, Sanctuary to the Virgin Mary and 17th-century church.

Poniec. The 19th-century Town Hall.

*Kalisz. Part of the façade
of the Town Hall built in the early 20th century.*

regulations and high taxes for Polish landowners were designed to ensure the speediest possible takeover of their assets by Germanic newcomers. In opposition to this, the keeping of land in Polish hands became a patriotic duty – and one that could only be achieved through outstanding management based on mechanisation and the latest cultivation techniques. It is probably for this reason that the farming in Wielkopolska was later to earn its reputation as Poland's most advanced.

*Sulmierzyce is a town on the Leszczyńska
Plateau. The arcaded wooden town hall from
1743 houses the Regional Museum.*

*Gołuchów boasts a 16th-century Renaissance castle
remodelled in the style of the French Renaissance in the
19th century and set in picturesque English-style parkland.*

*In Antonin, the wooden hunters' lodge from
the early 19th century has an exhibition room
devoted to Fryderyk Chopin.*

Konin. The Romanesque cross walled into the Gothic church.

The Sanctuary of Our Lady of Licheń Stary is the largest Catholic Church in Poland, built between the years 1994-2004; its architect was Barbara Bielecka.

Wielkopolska voivodship has a particularly noteworthy collection of old magnates' residences. A beautiful palace and park complex in **Kórnik**, for example, was last owned by Władysław Zamoyski, who gave it over to the nation in 1924. Today it houses a museum of interiors, with rich collections of furniture, paintings, sculptures and porcelain, as well as a library. **Rogalin** boasts a Rococo/Neo-Classical palace in parkland that includes **oaks** of girths

Licheń Stary. The miraculous likeness of the Licheń Mother of God.

Licheń Stary. Formed from erratic boulders left by the glaciers, the characteristic 25m Golgotha, Stations of the Cross and Licheń Sanctuary with custodian Father Eugeniusz Makulski.

*Made attractive by the presence of lakes, the **area around Konin** is a place of rest and relaxation for the inhabitants of the town itself.*

Pyzdry. *The garden of the square-shaped Franciscan monastery complex.*

in the range 7-9 m. The former coach-house has a collection of old coaches and carriages. Rydzyna is famous for its beautiful castle, while the park in Śmiełów rewards the visitor to the Neo-Classical palace complex with its museum devoted to Adam Mickiewicz. Memorabilia connected with the poet is gathered here, as are collections of European painting. In turn, an exceptionally original, Greek cross-shaped wooden hunting lodge can be seen in **Antonin**. Other interesting palaces and manors are to be found in **Pawłowice**, **Czerniejewo**, **Dobrzyca**, **Koszuty**, **Manieszki**, **Turew** and **Miłosław**. Surviving in Gołuchów is a castle that now presents collections of oriental and antique art. Further castles are to be found in **Koźmin**

Ciążeń. *The Rococo palace of the Bishops of Poznań. It holds the Poznań University Library with its collections of masonic literature.*

Miłosław. The 19th-century palace modeled on Italian villas and surrounded by a park.

Wielkopolski and in **Szamotuły**. Also of great historical value and beauty are some of the examples of religious architecture, like the monastery complex in **Ląd**, the sanctuary to the Virgin Mary in **Gostyń**, the monasteries or convents in **Koło**, **Kazimierz Biskupi** and **Pyzdry**, and the churches in **Kościan**, **Kościelec** and Piła. An exceptional place attracting pilgrims from throughout the country is **Licheń Stary**. Their goal is the painting of the Licheń Mother of God above the high altar in the Neo-Gothic church. In the sanctuary area, work is now coming to an end on **Poland's largest basilica**, which will have an internal volume of more than 300,000 m³.

Also within the voivodship, and not far from the city of Poznań, is the Wielkopolski National Park. This is augmented by several Landscape Parks and a number of reserves.

Czerniejewo. The conference room in the Baroque/Neo-Classical palace, which was restored after wartime devastation.

Trzemeszno. The interior of the Late Baroque church is topped off by a central polychromed dome.

Ląd. The Gothic ambulatory in the former Cistercian monastery complex.

Biechowo, whose Late Baroque monastery complex with its 15th-century Pieta makes this a place of piligrimage.

Gniezno. The 14th-15th century Gothic Cathedral of the Assumption of the Virgin Mary and St. Adalbert seen with Tumska Street.

Lednogóra. The 21 ha of the outdoor museum known as the Wielkopolska Ethnographic Park brings together buildings from all parts of "Greater Poland".

Sieraków is a resort on the Warta with several lakes just nearby.

Międzychód, a holiday resort for Poznań inhabitants. Market square houses.

9 LUBUSKIE
VOIVODSHIP (LUBUSZ)

Capital: **GORZÓW WIELKOPOLSKI**

This is one of Poland's smaller voivodships, covering less than 14,000 km². In the west it borders with Germany across the Nysa Łużycka and Oder Rivers. It takes in the eastern part of the **Lubusz Land** from history, with the remaining part – including the town of Lubusz itself – being German territory. Most of the present inhabitants of the Polish part are **descendents of settlers** brought in after 1945, since these lands were not Polish before the War. They came, in turn, from lands that were in pre-War Poland, but were ceded to the Soviet Union when hostilities ceased. The authorities sit in two centres, i.e. **Gorzów Wielkopolski** as the seat of the provincial

governor and **Zielona Góra** as the location of the elected regional assembly. Gorzów was founded in the mid 13th century, surrounded by strong fortifications and thus able to grow to become an important settlement in the Neumark region. A further flowering of the city came in the 18th century, as trade was enlivened by the completion of the **Bydgoszcz Canal.** This connected the Vistula and Oder basins. The oldest monument in Gorzów is its Gothic cathedral, while remnants of the defensive walls and granaries from the late 18th century are still to be found. Zielona Góra won its town rights in 1323, at which time it lay within the Dukedom of Głogów. At the beginning of the 16th century

Gorzów Wielkopolski. *Sunset on the Warta.*

Zielona Góra. The Old Market Square with its 17th-century Town Hall and view of the Mother of God of Częstochowa Church.

it was in turn part of the Czech lands for a couple of decades, before passing on to the Habsburgs. It became Prussian in 1742, and only came to Poland after the Second World War. The older parts include fine churches, parts of the city walls, and the Town Hall on the Old Market Square. Zielona Góra and its surroundings were famous for **vineyards** and the **production of wine**. Ten years ago, there were over 2000 vineyards, now there is only one – in the Park Winny.

Almost 50% of the voivodship's area is taken by forests. The largest blocks are the Drawska, Gorzowska, Notecka and Lubuska Forests, as well as the Dolnośląskie and Zielonogórskie Pine Forests. The greater part of the Drawieński National Park is within the limits of the region,

Zielona Góra was once famous for its vineyards and winemaking. Today there is only one left.

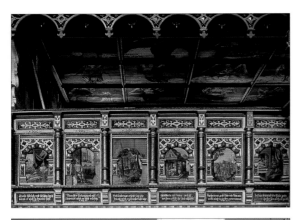

and there are also Landscape Parks and reserves. A large number of Monuments of Nature include the **huge oaks** in **Piotrowice** (with girths of 990 cm) and **Łęknica** (870 cm). **Świerkocin** has zoo with a safari motif, while the many lakes all have holiday centres. The most popular of all are **Lubniewice** and **Łagów**.

Many elements of the area's heritage are preserved. Żagan has one of **Poland's finest Baroque palaces**, as well as a formerly Augustine monastery complex. An interesting park plus palace is to be found in **Żary**, and there are castles in: **Łagów**, **Sulechów**,

Łagowiec. An old wooden chapel.

In the 18th century, **Sulechów** was famous for its clothmaking. The Town Hall standing on the Market Square has a 16th-century Neo-Gothic tower, while the tower of the more distant church is Late Gothic in style.

Ośno Lubuskie, an old historic town. The Gothic Parish Church.

Trzciel – a lakeside holiday centre with
the wooded banks of the River Obra.

Lubniewice is a centre for tourism and water-
based recreation by Lake Lubiąż.

Trzciel. Wickerwork
is a traditional lokal craft.

Międzyrzecz. In the Middle Ages, this was the fortified town
defending Wielkopolska against incursions from the west. Here
the remains of King Kazimierz the Great's castle.

The Międzyrzecz Fortified District. External remnants
of the fortifications include these reinforced concrete bunkers.

Kożuchów, Kostrzyn and **Międzyrzecz**, as well as small fortresses in **Lubniewice** and **Lubsko**. **Krosno Odrzańskie** preserves fragments of a castle of the Piasts, while **Sulechów** boasts not only a castle, but also stretches of the old ramparts, and a fine old town hall and church. **Międzyrzecz** also has a Neo-Classical town hall and Gothic church. Among the many surviving palaces those worthy of note include the ones in **Sława** and **Kargowa** as well as the one hidden among woodland in **Rogi**. **Szprotawa** has a church going back to the 18th century, as well as a town hall from a century later. Lovers of military architecture will in turn find the defences of the **Międzyrzecz Fortified District**

Żagań. Baroque church interior in the post-Augustian manastic complex.

of interest. These were erected by the Germans prior to World War II and are the largest of their kind in today's Poland. The underground passages are now home to **one of Europe's largest colonies of bats**.

Dębowa Łęka. Stork's nest, a common sight in Poland.

Wschowa is a historic town with Baroque architecture. From this corner we catch a glimpse of the Gothic-Renaissance Town Hall.

10 DOLNOŚLĄSKIE
VOIVODSHIP (LOWER SILESIA)

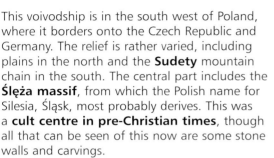

Capital: **WROCŁAW**

This voivodship is in the south west of Poland, where it borders onto the Czech Republic and Germany. The relief is rather varied, including plains in the north and the **Sudety** mountain chain in the south. The central part includes the **Ślęża massif**, from which the Polish name for Silesia, Śląsk, most probably derives. This was a **cult centre in pre-Christian times**, though all that can be seen of this now are some stone walls and carvings.

The voivodship capital, **Wrocław**, is one of Poland's oldest cities. In the year 1000, a bishopric subordinated to the Archbishopric of Gniezno was founded here. In turn, it was at the beginning of the 13th century that town rights were obtained. The destruction by the Tartars in 1241 and various changes of allegiance, notwithstanding, Wrocław never stopped developing. Only in the course of the Thirty Years' War and Silesian Wars was there any let-up in the growth. Wrocław became Prussian from 1763 and – as still a German city in World War II – was subject to **heavy Allied bombing**. Yet today's Wrocław is again a University city full of life and interesting historical buildings like the 14th-15th century **Gothic Town Hall**, the famous **Leopoldin Hall at the University** in the former Jesuit college, the 13th-15th century Gothic Cathedral of St. John and many other churches, monasteries

*The Old Town Market Square in **Wrocław** has this characteristic, richly-decorated Gothic Town Hall.*

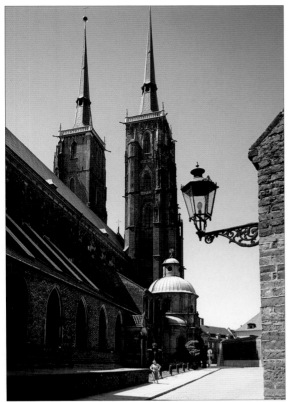

Wrocław, a settlement of the Slavic tribe
known as the Ślężanie in the first millennium.
Ostrów Tumski, St. John the Baptist's Cathedral.

The Baroque **Leopoldin Lecture Hall** built in 1732
to the design by Franz Joseph Mangoldt and Johann
Christoph Handke, as part of a **complex of buildings
that made up Wrocław University**.

and convents, tenement houses and palaces.
A particular attraction is the Battle of **Racławice
Panorama**, a painting by Jan Styka and
Wojciech Kossak which was produced in
1894 – the hundredth anniversary of this first
engagement in the Kościuszko Insurrection.
As a city on the River Oder, Wrocław has **over
100 bridges** over the main river and its
numerous branches. The best-known bridge of
all is the Grunwaldzki suspension bridge. The city
also boasts Poland's **largest and most famous
zoo**, which was founded in 1865.
Other large centres in the voivodship are

Oleśnica. The courtyard in the Castle of the Dukes
of Oleśnica, which was built of brick and stone
and has a cylindrical corner tower.

Legnica. The oft-rebuilt castle of the Piasts, large parts of whose walls are still standing.

Trzebnica. The Church of Sts. Bartholomew and Jadwiga. The sarcophagus of St. Jadwiga of Silesia was made from black and pink marbles in the years 1679-1680, along with the saint's likeness from white alabaster.

Stronia. The Early Gothic stone and brick church in rotunda form.

Jelenia Góra – Cieplice. Piatwoski Square with a view of the tower of the St. John the Baptist Church.

In **Mysłakowice**, alpine-style houses recall the former presence of several hundred settlers, while a monument honours their leader Johann Fleidl.

The **Milicz Ponds** – established in the late 13th and early 14th centuries for the breeding of fish, they are now a protected refuge for birds.

Świerzawa. The Romanesque Church of Sts. John the Baptist and Catherine. Part of a recently-discovered 14th-century mural on a wooden column of the gallery.

Bolków. A view of the historic town as seen from the partly-ruined castle.

Karkonosze. The Sudety Mountains are much visited by tourists drawn to their beautiful and unique landscape.

Legnica, Wałbrzych and Jelenia Góra.

In the place where Legnica now stands there was a Slavic defensive settlement as early as in the 8th century. Later on this was the capital of the Piast Dukedom of Legnica. The city has **Silesia's finest Baroque place of worship** – the church of John the Baptist, as well as the castle of the Dukes of Legnica, the Market Square with its Baroque Town Hall from the 18th century and tenement houses form the 16th. Wałbrzych was a place of industry from almost the start of its existence: **iron ore** was worked here as early as

Gross-Rosen, A monument and mausoleum on the site of the concentration camp set up close to Rogoźnica in 1940.

*The **Kaczawskie Hills** – a view from near Gostków.*

78

Henryków – the ex-Cistercian Church of the Assumption and St. John the Baptist. The ornate sculpturework of the interior was added during Baroque remodelling in the 17th century.

Strzegom is an important centre for the working of granite and basalt, with its still active quarry.

Strzegom. The interior of the Gothic-style Church of Sts. Peter and Paul has bas-relief stonework with epitaph plates among other things.

in the 14th century, coal from the 16th century on. Various heritage buildings remain, and some have museums. The now-closed "Julia" Mine houses the Museum of Industry and Technology, for example. Also within the city limits is the castle of the Hochbergs in **Książ**, which is **the largest in Lower Silesia**. Extending around the castle is a landscaped park renowned for its **rhododendrons**.

Świdnica. The Augsburg-Evangelical Church was erected in the years 1656-8. Thanks to the galleries, the Baroque interior seems more like that of a theatre than a church.

Będkowice – the archaeological reserve.

Kamieniec Ząbkowicki. The 19th-century Neo-Gothic castle was ruined as recently as in the post-War era.

Książ. The largest castle of the Piasts in Silesia, once a border fort, erected in the 13th century and rebuilt as recently as in the 19th century.

Jelenia Góra developed thanks to weaving and mining, but it owes its current popularity to tourism. Within its boundaries lies **Cieplice Śląskie-Zdrój** – a spa famous as early as in the Middle Ages. Other well-known health resorts in Lower Silesia are **Kudowa**, **Lądek**, **Polanica** and **Duszniki**.

Lower Silesia is famous for its many castles. Apart from the aforementioned one in Książ, there are better-known examples in places like **Głogów**, **Bolków**, **Grodziec**, **Oleśnica**, near Leśna (Czocha) and Sobieszów (**Chojnik**). There are also many old palaces, as at **Milicz**, **Wleń** and **Warmątowice**. Most localities retain some of

Wałbrzych. The Market Square with its restored burghers' houses.

Krzeszów. The polychromy on the ceiling of the Church of the Assumption, which is known as the "Pearl of the Silesian Baroque".

Szczawno Zdrój. A covered promenade in the spa well-known for its mineral waters.

their old architecture, often in the form of beautiful churches, market squares with town halls and stylish tenement houses, as at **Bystrzyca Kłodzka**, **Gryfów Śląski**, **Lądek Zdrój**, **Lwówek Śląski**, **Oława**, **Środa Śląska** and **Świdnica**. The many sacred buildings include the monasteries in Henryków, Kłodzko, Krzeszów, Lubiąż and Trzebnica, the Abbey in Kamieniec Ząbkowicki, and two well-preserved "Peace Churches" in Jawór and Świdnica, so-called because they were erected following the Thirty Years' War. A unique feature is the 13th-century **wooden Wang Chapel** in Karpacz, brought here from Norway in 1842.

Chełmsko Śląskie. An old complex of weavers' houses with both dwellings and places of work.

Also noteworthy is the sanctuary in **Wambierzyce** from the late 17th and early 18th centuries, known as the Silesian Jerusalem with its Stations of the Cross and almost 100 calvary shrines.
The greatest tourist hotspots in the region are the Karkonosze Mountains. Many trails make this a paradise for walkers, and the **Karkonoski National Park** is the centre of everything. Another interesting region is the Kłodzko Basin with its many sources of healing waters, as well as the Sowie Mountains – Poland's oldest, being

Kochanów. A mediaeval chair of judgment made of stone.

Błędne Skały – a landscape reserve with a rock labyrinth in the Stołowe Mountains.

Kłodzko. *The Gothic-style stone bridge has Baroque carvings of saints.*

__Bystrzyca Kłodzka__ is a town whose Mediaeval planning can still be seen. It is a centre of the match industry.

of Pre-Cambrian shales. Rather newer are the Second World War **tunnels** dug into them by the Nazis, some of which can be visited. The Stołowe ("Table") Mountains are also intriguing where the **rock forms take on a host of different shapes**. There is a National Park here too, as well as the famous **Błędne Skały** Nature Reserve.

The __Niedźwiedzia (Bear)__ Cave in the Sudety Mountains below Śnieżnik has Poland's best examples of stalactities and stalagmities.

Capital: **OPOLE**

This smallest of Poland's voivodships covers c. 9500 km². The north and central part is in the Silesian Lowland, with the part north of Opole being termed the Opole Plain. The Opawskie Hills lie in the south.

The history of these lands do not differ greatly from those of neighbouring Lower Silesia. Like other Silesian fiefs, the Dukedom of Opole was a Czech district under the Habsburgs, before it passed on to Prussia. A large number of the people living here are still **of German origin**, hence the lobby for the voivodship to be created in the first place. They have their own schools, organisations and members of parliament.

However ethnic Czechs and Ukrainians also live here.

The voivodship capital is **Opole**, which was founded at the beginning of the 13th century where an even older defended settlement had stood. The Old Town here is of interest, surrounded by Baroque tenement houses, and there is a Gothic Cathedral, the remains of the ramparts and the Piastowska Tower surveying all of them. Opole is famous for the **Song Festival** organised every year, while a further dose of atmosphere (of "**Little Venice**") is imparted by the picturesque buildings along a branch of the Oder called the Młynówka.

Opole, with old houses by the Młynówką, one of the branches of the Oder.

Opole. A likeness of St. Joseph on the corner of a building in Katedralna St.

Opole is the capital of Opole-Silesia. Here 16th-century tenement houses along the southern elevation of the Market Square.

Moszna near Opole has an Eclectic-style castle built at the end of the 19th century.

The second largest urban area is that of **Kędzierzyn-Koźle**, which emerged in 1975 with the linking of the four towns of Kędzierzyn, Koźle, Kłodnica and Sławęcice. Another quite large and significant town is **Nysa**, which remains one of Silesia's **most beautiful places**, despite the destruction wrought in World War II. The Old Town represents Opole-Silesia's finest built heritage.

Like Nysa, many of the region's other towns came through the War with monuments intact. One such place is **Brzeg**, with its Renaissance castle nicknamed **Silesia's Wawel**, the Piast school building from 1564, the **most precious Renaissance Town Hall in Silesia** and churches. Similar is **Głogówek**, with its Old

Namysłów. The neglected courtyard of the old castle with its Late Renaissance well.

Brzeg. Silesia's most beautiful Renaissance Town Hall.

Brzeg. The Renaissance castle sometimes called "Silesia's Wawel" has a courtyard gate with a richly-decorated entrance facade.

Małujowice. St. James's Church is adorned with Mediaeval murals.

Town and Town Hall, churches and ruined castle. **Paczków** is in turn famous for its Gothic town walls with 19 towers and 4 gates, as well as the Gothic fortified church, with that most necessary of items in a siege, a well **inside**. **Otmuchów** retains its Renaissance castle with the so-called horse steps. The city is also known for its annual flower festival. South of Opole is **Moszna**, with

Strzelniki. A section of Mediaeval polychromy within St. Anthony's Church.

Obórki. The Church of Sts. Peter and Paul is from the late 16th and early 17th centuries.

Kotórz Wielki. Not far from Opole, this village near Lake Turawskie boasts the Late Baroque Church of St. Michael the Archangel.

Głogówek. The Renaissance Town Hall with its highly ornate tops with carved saints on the corners.

its Eclectic palace and stud farm full of English bloodlines. One of Opole-Silesia's most important monuments is in turn the wonderful example of **Gothic polychromy** in the interior of **Małujowice** church. Also of note is the untypical wooden place of worship in **Oleśno**, which was raised to a design based on a five-petalled flower. To the south-east of the region's capital is a famous sanctuary of **Saint Anne's Mountain**. Once the site of a pagan cult, this now has a Baroque monastery with a calvary and 30 shrines. In consequence it has long been **the most important place of pilgrimage in Silesia**.

Paczków. A view of the old Church of St. John the Evangelist with the famous defensive walls around the town.

Otmuchów. The castle mound with its Baroque church and castle remodelled in the Renaissance period.

Nysa. The Late Gothic Church of Sts. James and Agnes.
The interior has three aisles of uniform height with cross
and star vaulting.

Nysa. The interiors of the Baroque palace house a museum.
The pearl of the painting collection is "Judith with the Head
of Holofernes" attributed to Lucas Cranach the Elder.

Prudnik. The 18th-century Town Hall was rebuilt.
Beside it is a Baroque-style well.

12 ŚLĄSKIE
VOIVODSHIP (SILESIA)

Capital: **KATOWICE**

This **most industrialised** of Poland's voivodships covers 12,300 km² and is inhabited by no fewer than 4.9 million people. This makes it the **most densely-populated region** in Poland. It borders with the Czech Republic and Slovakia to the south. The heavy industries to have been developed most strongly here are mining (for hard coal), steelmaking, the machinery industry and chemicals. The major aggregation of industry is in the Upper Silesian Industrial District, as well as around **Bielsko-Biała**, **Rybnik** and **Częstochowa**.
Katowice is the capital, and at the same time one of Silesia's youngest urban centres (it only obtained town rights in 1865). It appeared with

the dynamic development of industry in the 19th century, and its centre features a **Monument to the Silesian Uprisings** of 1919, 1920 and 1921. An unusual area worth a visit is the **Nikiszowiec** quarter of the city – an example of an early working-class housing estate. Other large centres of the Upper Silesian Industrial District are: **Chorzów**, **Sosnowiec**, **Dąbrowa Górnicza**, **Bytom**, **Zabrze**, **Tychy** and **Gliwice**. In **Tarnowskie Góry**, the "Black Trout" workings of an 18th-century silver mine can be visited by **boating along the flooded tunnels**. **Zabrze** in turn attracts visitors with its museum of the mining industry at the site of the Queen Luiza mine first

Katowice. *This old building from 1899 in the centre of the city was once the Royal High School, and remains a school to this day.*

Katowice. The Monument to the Silesian Uprisers was unveiled in 1967.

worked in 1791 and now of course closed. Chorzów boasts **Poland's largest Recreational Park** – whose 600 ha include a planetarium, National Stadium, large fairground, centre for water sports, a swimming-pool complex, a chairlift, light railway and zoo, as well as an ethnographic park with an open-air museum devoted to the Upper Silesian countryside. The most beautiful examples of architectural heritage are in **Będzin** (the castle), **Cieszyn** (the 11th-century Romanesque rotunda,

Katowice. A 32-metre cross honours the miners of the Wujek Mine who fell in the struggle for democracy of 1981.

Toszek. Erected in the 15th century, the Castle of the Dukes of Racibórz and Opole fell into ruin during the 19th century. It was partially rebuilt after World War II.

Będzin – the 14th-century Castle is now a District Museum.

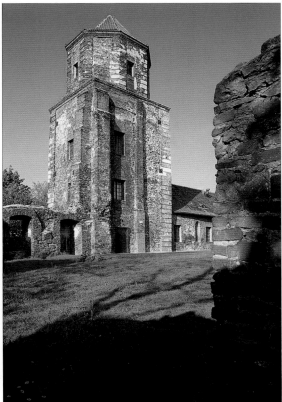

Pszczyna. The neo-Baroque Town Hall dating back to 1930, with the adjacent Evangelical Church in the same style.

Pszczyna. The collection of hunting trophies in the neo-Baroque palace of the Hochbergs. The Castle Museum presents residential interiors of the Renaissance period through to the 19th century.

*A member of the "Śląsk" Song and Dance Ensemble in the local dress of the **Cieszyn region**.*

*The orchestra of the **"Śląsk"** folk ensemble under the direction of the late Stanisław Hadyna, the group's long-time founder and inspirer.*

Cieszyn. A historic tenement house in Głęboka Street.

Żywiec. The late 14th-century Church of the Holy
Cross was remodeled in the 17th century.

churches, Old Town market square and Town Hall
and Gothic style defensive tower), **Pszczyna**
(Old Town, palace and outdoor museum),
Szczekociny (18th-century Baroque palace),
Żywiec (castle with arcaded courtyard) and
Bielsko-Biała (15th-century castle, Eclectic-style
Town Hall, other Secessionist-style buildings).
The voivodship also includes Poland's most
famous sanctuary to the cult of the Virgin Mary
with its miraculous likeness of the Mother
of God, namely the **Jasna Góra Monastery
in Częstochowa**. Another religious centre
of particular significance to Silesians
is Piekary Śląskie.

The **Beskid Śląski** range is a densely-forested
area put to intensive tourist use.

Złoty Potok. *The museum devoted to Zygmunt Krasiński in the single-storey Neo-Classical manor house of the Krasiński family.*

Ogrodzieniec. *The ruins of the Gothic-Renaissance fort are among Poland s largest (volume 32,000 m³).*

*Interesting geological formations – rocks near **Złoty Potok**.*

Mirów. *Ruins of the Gothic castle erected in the 14th-century reign of Kazimierz the Great.*

Pilica. *The castle ramparts.*

Perhaps surprisingly, the voivodship includes areas of natural beauty also – part of the **Kraków-Częstochowa** Upland, as well as the Silesian, Żywiec and Small Beskid ranges. The upland supports an interesting tourist path known as the **"Eagles' Nests" Trail**, which links the mediaeval fortresses of Olsztyn, Mirów, Bobolice and Ogrodzieniec, as well as the Jura Fortresses Trail. Olsztyn (near Częstochowa) also has annual outdoor festivals with **firework displays** and various performances. Popular centres in the aforementioned Beskids include the ski resorts of **Szczyrk, Korbielów, Wisła, Ustroń** and **Brenna**. Istebna and **Koniaków** are in turn villages famed for their **folk crafts**, e.g. lacekmaking.

Częstochowa. The outside altar at the top of the Jasna Góra Basilica.

Częstochowa. The miraculous Madonna of Jasna Góra wears a diamond robe – a unique testament to the jeweller's art.

13 ŚWIĘTOKRZYSKIE
VOIVODSHIP

Capital: **KIELCE**

This small voivodship of 11,700 km² supports c. 1.3 million inhabitants. A region lying between the Rivers Vistula and Pilica and known as the **land of Kielce**, it was the northern part of the historical Małopolska and was always of great significance in Polish history. The Slav tribe known as the Vistulanians had their state here as early as in the 9th century, becoming Christians around 880, or some 86 years before the baptism of Poland's Mieszko I. The Vistulanians came within the state established by Mieszko in the year 990.

The Kielce area has an ancient industrial tradition. In the Neolithic period, Krzemionki near Ostrowiec Świętokrzyski had **the largest quarries for flint used in the making of tools**. In turn, in the first millennium A.D. there was **Europe's largest centre producing iron** here (with some 300,000 ovens known as dymarki having been found). Copper, silver and lead used in the manufacture of coins were worked here in the Middle Ages, and later also marbles and sandstones fashioned by the area's famous stoneworks. This was also an area of 19th-century metallurgy known as the Staropolskie Industrial District. To this day, marbles, limestones, gypsums, sandstones, white clays, ores and glassmaking sands are worked in the area. It is also from the **Kielce** area that many types of **semi-precious stones** used in

Kielce. The well-preserved 17th-century Palace of the Bishops of Kraków now houses the National Museum.

jewellery are obtained. In connection with all this, it is not surprising that a dynamic development of industry here in the 19th century encouraged the establishment of Poland's first technical school, the Szkoła Akademiczno-Górnicza (Academic Mining School).

Kielce, a city in the hands of the Bishops of Kraków between the 11th and late 18th centuries, is the capital and main industrial settlement of Świętokrzyskie voivodship. Standing in memory of the former owners there is the lovely **Bishop's Palace**, considered the most beautiful piece of architectural heritage in the city. A second, similarly valuable building is the Baroque Cathedral, with still-surviving elements of the older Romanesque place of worship that came before it. Other large towns or cities in the

*A field with poppies in the **Chęciny area**.*

Jaskinia Raj – *one of Poland's most beautiful caves, it has a wealth of stalactites and stalagmites.*

Chęciny. *On the castle mound are the ruins of the fortress where Władysław the Short had his exchequer. It fell into this state in the wake of destruction wrought by the Swedes.*

region are: **Ostrowiec Świętokrzyski, Sandomierz, Starachowice** and **Skarżysko Kamienna**. The oldest place on this list is **Sandomierz**, a walled township as early as in the 10th century and one of Poland's most important centres just a century later. Standing as testimony to this history to the present day is the **Market Square with Renaissance Town Hall and tenement houses**, the Gothic cathedral rebuilt in the Baroque period, the Dominican priory and much else. Other parts preserve history equally well, as sacred architecture (e.g. the **Wąchock** Romanesque-Gothic Cistercian Abbey complex; the **Święty Krzyż** Benedictine Monastery erected on the site of an **old pagan**

*A roadside cross in **Krzcięcice**, a small village in the Kielce region.*

sanctuary; and Święta Katarzyna) and as temporal buildings (like the palace in **Kurozwęki**, town walls in Szydłów, and open-air museum in **Tokarnia**). Industrial heritage of various ages is also present (a flint quarry in **Krzemionki**, primitive iron kilns in **Nowa Słupia**, and what is left of an early 19th-century ironworks in **Samsonów**). Other heritage attesting to the former wealth of the region takes the form of the ruins of the large **Krzyżtopór** Castle in **Ujazd** once famous for its affluence. Towering above **Chęciny** are the ruins of another castle for a while belonging to the Kings of Poland.

The northern part of the voivodship is in the Kielce-Sandomierz Upland, of which the highest part is taken by the **Świętokrzyskie**

Tokarnia. Folk carvings in the open-air museum.

Nowy Korczyn. The brick-built, formerly Franciscan, Church of St. Stanisław, remodelled in the spirit of the Baroque.

Święty Krzyż. The ambulatory in the monastery.

Święty Krzyż. *East of Kielce, in the Łysa Góra Massif, is a Benedictine Abbey funded by King Bolesław Wrymouth in the 12th century.*

Wąchock. *The interior of the Late Romanesque St. Florian's Church was once part of a Cistercian Abbey.*

Mountains. This is a very attractive area for tourists, full of interesting places, well-marked trails and mysterious caves (**the "Paradise Cave" Jaskinia Raj is open to visitors**). Nature is protected in the Świętokrzyski National Park and a large number of reserves. The southern part of the region in the Nida Trough is famous for the curative properties of its waters, and there are famous spas in **Busko Zdrój** and **Solec Zdrój**. There are also Monuments of Nature, of which the **"Bartek" oak** is Poland's most famous.

Staszów *was famed for its weaving and pottery in the 16th century. A Monument to Tadeusz Kościuszko stands in the Market Square.*

Sandomierz is situated on elevations of loess by the Vistula. Here a view of the old town with its Baroque St. Michael's Church.

Sandomierz. The preserved west wing of the 15th-century Royal Castle houses the District Museum.

Ujazd – The Krzyżtopór Family castle. The Mannerist construction from the years 1627-1644 lay in ruins as early as in 1656 – having been put to the torch by the invading Swedes.

14 LUBELSKIE (LUBLIN) VOIVODSHIP

Capital: **LUBLIN**

This eastern voivodship covers more than 25,000 km², and takes in both the traditional **Lublin region** and parts once included within Małopolska, Mazowsze, Podlasie and Ruthenian Halicz (Chełm). Most of what is today included was already within the confines of Mieszko I's Poland.

The seat of the voivodship is **Lublin**, which has been in possession of its town charter since 1317. There was a defensive settlement of some significance here at least a century earlier, however, with the first traces of occupation going back to the 6th century. It was here in

1569 that the General Parliament was convened and the Lublin Union between Poland and Lithuania proclaimed. Lublin was already a major commercial and cultural centre at the time, though it was to fall later in the wars with Sweden. Renewed development on a major scale had to wait for the mid 19th century, while the Second World War saw the city's environs blighted by the establishment of the Nazis' **Majdanek Concentration Camp**.

The c. 360,000 people murdered there are remembered in a sombre monument, while the camp itself is a museum.

Lublin. The Holy Trinity Chapel in the castle is Gothic in style, and preserves Russian-Byzantine polychromy from the early 15th century.

Lublin. The façade of the 14th-century Castle remodeled in the neo-Gothic style in the early 19th century.

Nałęczów is a spa for the treatment of cardiac ailments thanks to its mild lowland climate and healing waters.

Back with Lublin city and happier things, the characteristic building is the Royal Castle with its **Gothic Holy Trinity Chapel** wherein the priceless Russo-Byzantine polychromy was funded by Władysław Jagiełło. A further major monument is the Old Town complex, with its Town Hall and wonderful churches set among picturesque tenement houses.

The region's other larger centres are **Zamość**, **Chełm**, **Biała Podlaska** and **Puławy**, each boasting its own interesting history. Zamość is rather **unique with its all-of-a-piece Renaissance plan**, 17th-century Mannerist-Baroque Town Hall and Market Square set about with arcaded tenement houses – all the idea of Commander-in-Chief of the Army (Hetman) Jan

Wojciechów near Nałęczów. The habitable "Ariańska" tower of the old castle. Interiors include a Museum of Smithery.

Kazimierz Dolny. Richly-decorated tenement houses from 1615.

Zamoyski from 1580, as well as the work of architect Bernardo Morando. In turn, **Chełm** was the 13th-century capital of Ruthenian Halich, coming within Polish territory from 1366 on. **Biała Podlaska** was the property of the wealthy Radziwiłł family for 250 years from the mid 16th century onwards. Many surviving buildings and monuments from that time attest to the wealth of both family and town. The Academy opened here in 1628 was a higher education establishment which left Biała an important scientific and cultural centre of Podlasie from the 17th century.

Puławy is in turn best known for its palace and park, as is **Kozłówka**, a locality c. 40 km north of Lublin. No less interesting are the palaces and manors in **Kock**, **Lubartów**, **Radzyń Podlaski**

Kazimierz Dolny is a picturesquely-located resort town above the Vistula boasting a Renaissance town plan. Here the Market Square and parish church.

Puławy. The Neo-Classical Temple of Sybil in the Palace Park was modelled on the Temple of the Vestal Virgins in Tivoli.

Kozłówka. Rebuilt in the Neo-Baroque style, the Zamoyski Palace has an impressive museum of interiors.

Lubartów. The 17th-century palace of the Sanguszko family stands in extensive parkland.

and **Rejowiec**. In **Zwierzyniec**, an attraction in addition to the palace is the "Church on the water", while **Nałęczów**, which has been a well-known spa for years, boasts the Old Bath House. A particular place on the map of Poland is **Kazimierz Dolny**, a town of exceptional atmosphere and charm. The market square is surrounded by **Renaissance-style tenement houses** overlooked from on high by the ruins of a castle with a 14th-century Gothic tower. Hardly surprising that this is a **mecca for artists**. The places of worship of a number of different faiths can be found in the region: Catholic

*The rural landscape in **Starościn** near Kozłówka.*

. *The Late-Renaissance St. Anne's Church is a sanctuary with a miraculous likeness of the Mother of God known as the Queen and Mother of Podlasie.*

Wola Okrzejska. *The single-storey wooden manor house from the early 19th century is the birthplace of Henryk Sienkiewicz. Today it is a museum devoted to the Nobel Prizewinning author.*

Leśna Podlaska *has a Paulite monastery complex and Sanctuary to the Virgin Mary. The Chapel has a well regarded as miraculous.*

churches, Orthodox churches – especially in the eastern part – and synagogues in such places as **Szczebrzeszyn**, **Włodawa** and Zamość. Nature in this region has been brought under protection inter alia in two National Parks centred on the Polesie marshlands and Roztocze Hills, as well as in numerous Landscape Parks and Nature Reserves.

Biała Podlaska. *The wooden vicarage from the 19th century on the site of St. Anne s Parish Church.*

The Bug. This picturesque and unregulated river is a tributary of the Vistula. It forms Poland's eastern border along a significant part of its length.

Zamość, known as the "Padua of the North", was designed by Italian architect Bernardo Morando. On the northern elevation of the Great Market Square is the Renaissance Town Hall with built-on Baroque stairs.

Zamość. The two-storey arcaded tenement houses recall Italian architecture.

15 PODKARPACKIE
VOIVODSHIP

Capital: **RZESZÓW**

Lying in the south-eastern corner of Poland, this voivodship borders with Ukraine to the east and Slovakia to the south. Industrialisation has been limited here, though sulphur is mined near Tarnobrzeg, while deposits of natural gas are also present. Considerable parts of the voivodship are taken by the Eastern Beskids and Bieszczady Mountains, as well as the Low Beskids and Beskid Foreland. Abandoned by many of its inhabitants after the War, the wild **Bieszczady Mountains** earn many admirers with their unspoilt nature and limited numbers of visitors. Well-prepared trails for walkers and tracks for mountain bikers and skiers can be enjoyed in peace here. The mountain views can also be taken in from a horse's back and the visitor can even partake in a cowbowy-like cattle roundup. A National Park was established in the Bieszczady in 1973, and this now covers 27,800 ha. It also forms part of the Eastern Carpathians International Biosphere Reserve, along with adjacent protected areas in Ukraine and Slovakia. The voivodship also boasts the greater part of the Magurski (Magura) NP, which includes the most precious parts of the Low Beskids. Several Landscape Parks and a host of Nature Reserves complete the lineup of protected areas.

Rzeszów is a town on the Wisłok. Here the Market Square with its Eclectic 19th-century Town Hall and Monument to Tadeusz Kościuszko.

Rzeszów. The Lubomirski's castle is a 19th-century building atop 17th-century fortifications.

Piaseczno. *The interesting landscape in what was once a sulphur mine.*

Baranów Sandomierski. *The arcaded courtyard of the 16th-17th century Mannerist castle.*

The region retains **populations of various faiths and origins**: there are Poles, Lemko people and Ukrainians – hence the presence here of many Russian Orthodox and Greek Catholic churches, as well as Roman Catholic ones. There were many Jews here too, before the War, but all that tells of their presence now are old cemeteries and synagogues.

The capital of the Podkarpackie voivodship is **Rzeszów** – a city founded in 1354 on the site of an old fortified township from the Middle Ages. From 1772 on, the city was in the part of the country partitioned off by Austria, only returning to Poland in 1918. The most important piece of architectural heritage in Rzeszów is the

Łańcut. *The beautiful 17th-century park has a two-storey castle remodelled in the French neo-Baroque style.*

Bernardine Church of the Assumption from the first half of the 17th century. The province's very interesting second city is **Przemyśl**, which was a township as early as in the 10th century, having probably been settled first in the 2nd century B.C. In the scond half of the 19th century A.D., the city took on a formidable appearance as **towers and forts** were erected. Nevertheless, much old construction remains, especially in the Old Town with its 15th-16th century cathedral, remodelled in the Baroque style. Fine castles may also be visited at **Krasiczyn**, **Łańcut** and **Baranów Sandomierski**. Krasiczyn is around 10 km west of Przemyśl. Its imposing

Sieniawa. The Baroque palace of the Sieniawski family with the Kościuszko apartment.

Dubiecko. The 16th-century Manor is now the Igancy Krasicki Museum.

Renaissance-Mannerist style castle set in landscaped parkland is one of **Poland's most beautiful** and was built in stages between 1592 and 1618. Of a rather different character is Łańcut Castle, a **splendid magnate's residence** from the 17th century which currently presents its Neo-Baroque French style. The old coach-house building now houses the **Museum of Horse-drawn Transport**. Łańcut is famous for its festival of serious music. Another Museum – of Interiors (mainly from the 16th and 17th centuries), and **Poland's only sulphur museum** are to be found in Baranów Sandomierski in a castle dating back to the years

__Krasiczyn__. The Renaissance-Mannerist Castle of the Krasickis in a park from the 19th century.

*The **Solińskie Reservoir** was created by the damming of the San and is a major centre for watersports.*

The **Western Bieszczady Mountains**. The renowned and much-visited massif of Połonina Wetlińska, which peaks at 1255m Roh.

Lesko. The Late Renaissance building of the old synagogue was reconstructed in the years 1960-1963.

1591-1606. Romantics and lovers of antiquities should stop of at **Sieniawa**, in an unusual hotel formed from a beautiful Baroque palace surrounded by parkland, which was laid out in the late 17th and early 18th centuries. In **Leżajsk**, the Bernardine church has **one of Poland's finest and most famous organs**, which forms the centrepiece of the town's international festivals of organ music. Bóbrka is also worth a visit, as a cradle of the world's oil industry. The Ignacy Łukasiewicz Open Air Museum takes its name from the discoverer of the oil refining process and **inventor of the oil lamp**.

Krempna.The old Orthodox (now Catholic) church from the late 18th century is of wood.

Haczów. "The Coronation of the Mother of God" is polychromy dating back to 1494 and still preserved in the chancel of what is the largest Gothic church in wood, and also one of the oldest (not only in Poland).

16 MAŁOPOLSKIE
VOIVODSHIP (LESSER POLAND)

Capital: KRAKÓW

This voivodship takes in an area very diverse from the points of view of relief, industrialisation, tradition and folklore. The present-day administrative boundaries correspond quite closely with those of the historical **Małopolska** ("Little Poland"), regarded as one of the core areas of Polish statehood, and encompassing the Małopolska Upland, as well as most Polish parts of the Carpathians, and the Sandomierz and Oświęcim Depressions (Sandomierz itself is now within Lublin voivodship). It is through this region that trading routes from Western Europe through to the Black Sea ran, and this favoured the development and enrichment of the area, as did mining for salt and metal ores.

The seat of today's voivodship and the Małopolska of old is **Kraków**, a city that was already of major political significance by the end of the 10th century. A Bishopric was created here in the year 1000, and the first Cathedral erected on the Wawel Hill. Though city status was not in fact obtained until 1257, Kraków had been the **preferred residence of the monarchs** from the mid 11th century on. It became the official capital in 1320, when Władysław Łokietek ("the Short") was crowned in the Wawel Cathedral. Forty-four years later,

Kraków. *The Main Market Square with Cloth Hall and Gothic St. Mary's Church.*

Kraków. In St. Mary's Church, one of the scenes on Veit Stoss Gothic altar of 1477-1489 portrays the "Descent of the Holy Ghost".

Kraków, The Wawel Cathedral of Sts. Wacław and Stanisław the Bishop. The characteristic domes are of the Waza and Zygmuntowska Chapels.

Oświęcim (Auschwitz) is a name that still chills. The several million people killed here in World War II make what is today a museum a potent symbol of the Holocaust.

King Kazimierz the Great founded the **Krakow Academy – Poland's first higher education establishment**. The period of real flowering of the city continued until the end of the 16th century, with culture, architecture, all forms of art and learning flourishing. Many foreign artists and teachers came here to live. However, the transfer of the royal residence to Warsaw in the late 16th and early 17th centuries marked the

Brzezinka (Birkenau) – was a sub-camp of the main concentration camp in Auschwitz; it is now a museum.

Alwernia in Rudniański Landscape Park.

Rudno. The ruins of the 14th-century Knights' Castle in Tenczyn.

onset of a slow but sure decline of Kraków, even if this was still the place of coronation and royal burial.

World War II left the city relatively intact in the material sense – its architectural heritage remained in place. However, the people which made the city so special were not spared, as the Nazis murdered all the professors and scientific employees in higher education.

Today, while Warsaw is undoubtedly the capital, it is still for many Kraków that is the country's most important cultural and educational centre. It also represents the most important complex of monuments, entered on the World Heritage List run by UNESCO.

Wadowice, birthplace of Karol Wojtyła or Pope John Paul II. The cream cakes of childhood recalled by His Holiness on his last visit here are now to be bought all over the town.

A further curiosity, also a World Heritage Site, is the **Wieliczka Salt Mine**, with its beautiful chambers, sculptures and even chandeliers carved out of the rock salt. The Chapel of St. Kinga is perhaps the finest chamber of all, while the mine also operates a sanatorium for respiratory and rheumatic diseases some 200 m below the surface.

In a well-preserved state and usually open to visitors are the castles in **Niepołomice**, **Niedzica**, **Nowy Wiśnicz**, **Pieskowa Skała** and **Sucha Beskidzka**. **Szymbark** in turn has a quite unsual fortified manor. Many of the towns of Małopolska also retain their original urban plan plus many old buildings. Examples here might be **Nowy Sącz**, **Tarnów** and **Stary Sącz**. Many

Ojcowski (Ojców) National Park – *is one of the country's smallest. With a prevalence of broadleaved trees it looks beautiful in autumn.*

Pieskowa Skała. This limestone rock c. 25 m tall is named Hercules's Club.

Pieskowa Skała. One of Poland's largest castles from the age of chivalry.

interesting contemporary buildings are also to be seen up and down the region, including the **painted wooden architecture typical of Podhale**, as exemplified in such villages as Zalipie. A must-see of a quite different kind more likely to generate reflection, deep sadness or even horror is the museum on the site of the former Nazi extermination camp of **Auschwitz-Birkenau** in Oświęcim.

However, it is not merely history and buildings that make this the most-visited part of Poland. The **Tatra**, **Pieniny** and **Beskidy Mountains** are all here, plus the **Kraków-Częstochowa Upland**, and hence a wealth of nature protected

Książ Wielki. Standing on the hill is the palace erected in the late 16th century and later remodelled in the Neo-Gothic English style.

Wieliczka. The old castle houses the Museum of the Kraków Salt Mine, while the Neo-Classical Church of St. Clement is just nearby.

in 6 National Parks. The Tatra Mountains draw fans of alpine tourism, climbing and winter sports, while the area's National Park combines with the adjacent Park in Slovakia to form an International Biosphere Reserve. Nearby **Zakopane** is **Poland's "winter capital"**, combining with other localities in Podhale to offer a fine accommodation base. Skiers are otherwise well provided for by the large number of lifts and runs. The Pieniny Mountains are in turn renowned for the **picturesque gorge of the Dunajec,** in which organized rafting trips allow visitors to enjoy the scenery at close quarter. The Pieniński National Park was founded

Nowy Wiśnicz. The castle is a Baroque-styled fortified residence with corner towers and surrounding bastions.

Niepołomice – the Renaissance-style royal hunting palace with its cloistered courtyard.

Zalipie – is "the painted village". Each year, Corpus Christi day brings a contest for the most beautifully-painted house.

Nowy Sącz, situated in a basin, has an Eclectic late 19th-century Town Hall in the centre of its market square

Dębno – the 15 th century wooden church of St. Michael.

Ludźmierz is regarded as the oldest village in the Podhale region (from the early 13th century) – it is famous for its miraculous likeness of the Mother of God.

here, while the region's other National Parks centre on Mt. Babia Góra and the Gorce Mountains, as well the Magura Hills (shared with the Podkarpackie voivodship) and the Ojców Hills, where fine examples of the limestone landscape of the Kraków-Częstochowa Upland are protected. A particular attraction of the Ojcowski NP are its more than 200 caves.

In *Zubrzyca Górna*, the Orava region Ethnographic Park features hut interiors.

Stary Sącz has retained its Mediaeval town plan to this day. Its Market Square has remained paved with field cobblestones.

Łopuszna. *The wooden manor of the Tetmajer family now houses the Museum of the Nobility.*

Niedzica. *The Gothic-Renaissance fortress as seen from the dam on the Dunajec.*

The **Pieniny Mountains**. *A raft ride through the picturesque gorge of the Dunajec.*

Zakopane. *Towering above the town is the characteristic outline of Giewont.*

Kuźnice. *The cable car up to Kasprowy Wierch was built in the years 1935-1936, making it one of the oldest operating systems in Europe.*

Podhale. *A colourful Corpus Christi procession.*

Zakopane. *The chapel in Jaszczurówka, built in 1908, was designed in the so-called Zakopiański style by Stanisław Witkiewicz.*

Eighteen localities in Małopolska have spa or health-resort status, with the most popular places to take a cure being **Rabka**, **Krynica**, **Szczawnica** and **Muszyna**. There are also two important Catholic sanctuaries **Kalwaria Zebrzydowska**, and the nearby **Wadowice**, birthplace of Karol Wojtyła – better known as Pope John Paul II.

Zakopane. *Krupówki Street is the town's main pedestrian precinct. In summer it is filled with café gardens and holidaying crowds.*

The **Tatra Mountains**. The slope of Kasprowy Wierch up to Hala Gąsienicowa. The Świnica Massif (2300 m) dominates in the background.

The **crocus** is the harbinger and symbol of the Tatra spring.

The **Tatra Mountains**. The Siklawa Falls (c. 40 m high) are the most powerful and beautiful in the Tatras, and are situated at the upper end of the Roztoki Valley.

The Hostel by the **Morskie Oko** tarn in the High Tatras.

The **Tatra Mountains**. Rather resembling goats, chamois are classed in a separate family. They enjoy legal protection.

POLAND

CHRISTIAN PARMA */photography*

RENATA GRUNWALD-KOPEĆ */text*

BOGNA PARMA */layout, captions to photographs, editor*

JAMES RICHARDS */translation*

Publishers PARMA PRESS
05 270 Marki, al. Józefa Piłsudskiego 189 b
+48 22/781 16 48, 781 16 49
e-mail: wydawnictwo@parmapress.com.pl
http://www.parmapress.com.pl

ISBN 978-83-7777-028-3